EARLY CANADIAN
ART AND LITERATURE

Early Canadian Art and Literature

A. Ch. v. GUTTENBERG, Ph.D.
University-Professor

EUROPE PRINTING ESTB.
VADUZ
LIECHTENSTEIN

First published in Great Britain by
Europe Printing Establishment
FL–9490 Vaduz,
Geschäfthaus Mercantil,
Landstrasse 856,
Fürstentum, Liechtenstein

Printed by the Barleyman Press, Bristol
Bound by the Pitman Press, Bath
using paper supplied by Frank Grunfeld Ltd.

To the memory of the pioneers
of two nations
who laid the foundations of
Canadian culture

CONTENTS

Preface	9
JOSEPH MARMETTE	20
WILLIAM KIRBY	34
OCTAVE CRÉMAZIE	45
CHARLES MAIR	63
MARIA CHAPDELAINE	83
SUSANNA MOODIE	99
CHARLES GILL	120
JAMES WILSON MORRICE	137
CORNELIUS KRIEGHOFF	148
Epilogue	168
Historical Table	171
Bibliography	172
Index of Names	173

PREFACE

It was in 1603 that the first settlers arrived from France and founded a little hamlet on the coast of what is now the Province of Nova Scotia. Five years later Samuel Champlain, proceeding inland, founded another little settlement consisting of a few log cabins walled in by palisades, on the north shore of the majestic river named after Saint Lawrence. The immense unexplored forests were hopefully called 'La Nouvelle France—New France'. In just over three hundred years this settlement has developed into the exciting city of Quebec.

Between 1608 and 1760 about 55,000 new immigrants arrived, most of them from the north-western provinces of France. They were peasants and simple people of the soil, hardly knowing how to read and write—which however, was nothing unusual in Europe at the time. What little education one could find, was represented by a few traders and adventurers who had joined the settlement hoping to make a fortune within a few years or sooner. On a higher level, the King's civil servants and the priests provided a measure of culture and knowledge shared by the better classes in Europe.

There are many reasons why literature and art developed only much later, during the second half of the nineteenth century. The foremost was the Seven Years' War, at the end of which (1763) the new colony 'La Nouvelle France'—amongst others—was ceded to Great Britain by the Bourbons. The political cession was accompanied by a 'liquidation of mind' in the colony to which Voltaire had sarcastically referred as 'a few useless acres of snow'. But even at that time this sarcasm was not completely justified, as is shown by a report presented to the Swedish Academy of Science, which describes Quebec and Montreal as elegant and progressive cities. For these cities, however, the cession was a near catastrophe, since a large part of the upper-class French population left the country, taking their capital with them, in order to get away from the military reign of the Britishers. This alone threatened to take Canada back to the stage of 'useless acres of snow' mentioned by Voltaire.

A new menace to the predominance of the French-Canadian language and religion was presented by the immigration of about 35,000 British Loyalists, most of them Protestants, who, after the Declaration of Independence of the Southern Colonies, preferred settlement in a British Crown Colony to the liberty of the American Republic. The possibility that the English-speaking population would, in time, represent a large majority, was prevented in the course of the years by the greater fecundity of the French-Canadians. Another important factor in the development of the country became evident after the influx of British capital. Even today the largest industrial corporations are in British hands, particularly paper mills and railways. Friction between English and French-Canadians was frequent and, in 1837, a heroic but vain uprising of the French-speaking population took place. All these events powerfully worked against the utilisation of energy for cultural development.

It has been fortunate that, for many years now, French-English controversy has diminished continually as a result of better understanding between the groups. This understanding has been fostered by the growth of Canadian national mind as opposed to concepts of origination, and by the gradual accumulation of wealth by French-Canadians. The final result is that the controversies have lost of their bitterness.

*   *   *

When judging Canadian art and literature it should be borne in mind that, up to now, no former European colony has attained to an independent level of these activities on a par

with the Mother-country. Literature and art being amongst
the later flowers of well-established European civilisations,
obviously they will also need long periods of development in
young countries. This not only refers to the French—but
equally to the English-speaking part of the population. So
much time is needed in Canada for heavy daily routines, and
so little time is left—as yet—for the production and contemplation of the arts. The problem of which internal and which
external values must be developed, and which fusions must
take place in the soul of a nation to produce the beautiful
mirror reflecting a civilisation of its own, has not yet been
entirely solved.

For Canada, however, there are two fundamental facts which
reveal that it is already well on the road towards an art and
literature of its own. On the one hand there is the growing
intellectual and spiritual separation from Great Britain, and
on the other the critical, independent attitude towards France.
The growing independence from the Mother-countries receives
considerable impetus from the development of a national
Canadian temperament and mind, which increasingly trans-
mutes former antagonisms into mutual esteem for the spiritual
and material values of the country. This development is aided
by the fact that many immigrants do not belong to either the
English- or the French-speaking part of the population. These
elements, having no ties with one or the other, are well inclined
to become simply 'Canadian'. At present they already represent 20 per cent. of the total population. In particular, the
more intelligent of these immigrants enjoy the assimilation of
two languages which are keys to two of the noblest civilisations
and cultures of European soil. This does not mean losing in
any way the values of their ethnical ancestry; on the contrary,
it means an addition to these values.

It is certainly no exaggeration to say that the intellectual
goodwill and the liberal mutual interpenetration referred to
above have created a set of new tools of rare value for the
production of works of art and in some way of literature. On
Canadian soil and with the background of the Canadian way

of life, two civilisations, represented by two different languages, are being fused to create a new world artist. Evidence that such a fusion may produce rare results has already been provided by the ancient Greek Diaspora, resulting in a most valuable contribution of Hellenic Thought, Philosophy, Literature and Art to the total of Man's culture.

I am well aware of the fact that this point of view is a challenge to the defenders of the dogmas of the exclusive development of culture, literature and art by a given nation, free from external mixtures. It would be well to remember that as far as these dogmas are concerned that modern anthropology as well as prehistoric anthropology has proven that all European peoples sprang from a common source and even such an extremist as Count Gobineau might have had to change some of his ideas had he been part of the Court of Charles the Great, or a visitor to the European Parliament at Strasbourg of today. We have learned enough, and we are at a sufficient distance from the mental dictatorship of the Encyclopedists, to know and assert that European nations are not pre-established facts of Nature. They do not perish only: they have to pass through a long process of birth and development. Both the French and the English nations, members of the Indo-European racial family, developed through bodily fusion of Celtic and Germanic elements, with one purely spiritual substance added: Latin and Greek civilisation. We are fully entitled to assume that a process of this kind does not stand isolated in the history of Mankind, and in particular in the history of Western Europe. History might repeat itself if—in case if the far-fetched dream of a United Europe came true—this sole State of Europe would look back critically on the history of its own development. The spiritual achievement of Hellenic thought (still underrated today), or the epic European literature of the period of Carolus Magnus (which at that time came very near to producing one State of Europe), show that tendencies such as we have mentioned were—and are—ever present in the history of the nations of Europe.

Moreover, they demonstrate that we are not confronted by a

lukewarm decanting of past civilisations, but by independent cultures with a pulsing life all their own. These civilisations are children of a very mixed ancestry, but this inheritance could never be used as an argument against the independence of their existence.

But we should not forget that French settlers were the first white immigrants in Eastern Canada and that their manners and morals were the first to cause an imprint on the customs of the wide area where they lived. It is important to remember that in contrast with the home country France, the French-Canadian does not know a separation of People and Church. Therefore the Church has always played an important role in the education of the French-Canadian. In their spiritual world of today, the Catholic Church has the privilege of being an exponent of a general culture derived from the ancient Greek-Latin synthesis, which is fully humanistic and fully alive. We may leave it to the reader to derive from all this his own perspective of the cultural, artistic and literary development of the French-speaking part of Canadians.

The same facts represent the only real bulwark against the increasing tendency of dollar-adoration imported from the United States. These facts are important since they present to a large extent the excessive increase of a special type of the 'homo sapiens americanus' which has no interests apart from financial success and industrial development. The danger of an overdose of materialism is perhaps stronger for the English-Canadian, who generally belongs to one of the many Protestant religious denominations and, unlike the French-Canadian, does not possess a language-barrier to American influence. The Jewish element, fairly strong in the big cities and engaged in the most diversified activities, performs the function of leaven in this interesting amalgamation of languages and religions.

Let us try to answer this fundamental question: what has actually happened in the field of independent culture, literature and art since the early days of the first settlers? It would be too great a simplification to imagine that such a development has taken place as one whole, and in one direction only. Reality is more likely to show a long campaign with advances and retreats, with the formation of a hinterland where you may find a consolidation of culture, and a fighting front which claims many victims. In 1635 you would have found that outside the gates of Quebec City war was being waged with Indian tribes and, simultaneously, the Jesuits inside the city were founding the first classical college. In the year 1749 Kalm forwarded a travel report to the Swedish Academy of Science, mentioning the fact that he found in Quebec 'a society of distinction which had preserved good taste, excellent manners and general culture, as was demonstrated by language and customs'. Moreover, Bougainville wrote that in 1757 Quebec already possessed a literary circle. It is therefore evident that the soil was already prepared for the blossoming of art and literature. The French-Canadians cannot be blamed for the fact that this development was frequently interrupted. The conquest of Canada by the British and the subsequent years of strife did not favour continuous development.

The efforts towards mutual understanding between both language groups started early, notwithstanding prolonged antagonism. The situation was highly unusual, as, on both sides, one hand was extended in friendship and understanding whilst the other was still the mailed fist, ready to strike. The explanation for this extraordinary state of affairs was that, on one hand, the oppositions inducing war were imported from overseas and originated in the past, whereas on the other the necessary conditions for the future development of Canada, disregarding original language or nation, induced understanding.

The first indications of such an understanding were also to be found in literature. Joseph Quésnel (1749–1809) immigrated from France, tells this story of understanding in his comedy 'Anglomanie'. English-speaking authors follow the same trend—obviously in accordance with the reading public —and many works appeared of which the action takes place in French-Canadian surroundings. We may mention in this conection a novel called 'The Golden Dog' by William Kirby (1877) which had a Quebec background, and also the poetry of William Dow-Lighthall and William Henry Drummond. The first Canadian historian, Michel Bibaud (1782–1857) was often criticised by his French compatriots to the effect that his 'History of Canada' was prejudiced in favour of the British Government. Of Bibaud, it is perhaps fair to say that he, too, tried to contribute towards mutual understanding.

This understanding gained ground very slowly, as it was hampered continuously by the battle waged for the future basis for cultural values. The battle is particularly prominent in French-Canadian literature, highly patriotic throughout as it was. One of the most noble exponents of patriotic poetry was the unfortunate Octave Crémazie (1827–1879), bookseller and poet. His 'Song of an Old Canadian Soldier' and other works revive the love of home and the fame of the old French-Canadians. English-Canadian literature of this epoch is of an entirely different nature: it shows resentment against the successful neighbours south of the Canadian frontier. Nevertheless, there is also poetry and prose which remains detached from current problems, of which Charles Sangster (1822–1893) provides an excellent example in 'The St. Lawrence, the Saguenay, and other Poems'.

It seems to be a rule that secondary cultures are able to show the flowers of literature before the fruits of painting, sculpture and music ripen to the same beauty. The literary expression of Canadian spiritual life seems to be best represented in the historical novel and national poetry, both of which start developing around the year 1840, in French as well as in English. The first of the historical patriotic novels in the English language was produced by the soldier John Richardson (1796–1852) under the title: 'Wacousta or the Prophecy; A Tale of Canada'. The first historical novel in French was written by Napoleon Bourassa (1827–1916), politician, artist and author, who called his work 'Jacques et Marie; Souvenir d'un peuple dispersé'. Also prominent in this field are Octave Crémazie, already mentioned, and Louis

Fréchette (1839–1908), the most productive, but not quite on the same level of poetic ability.

Nobody will deny that the form and language of all these products show a strong affinity with European patterns of the same period; as a matter of fact, only to be expected. The Canadian historical novel of this period reminds one of Alexandre Dumas; the poetry follows Victor Hugo. All this is true up to a point only, however, since all these novels and poems closely reflect typical personalities, landscapes and situations of Canadian life. Even today this is not sufficiently taken into account. As always, several generations will be needed to provide the necessary perspective to show that these works are Canadian literature, and not a plagiarism of European art.

In our own generation, the inheritor of a great past in art and literature, it seems impossible that they can still be created by one sole driving principle, or by one intuition, as occurred in old Hellas or at the beginning of the Dutch oil painting. Nowadays we have to reckon everywhere with inherited progressive developments. The development of science and industry has also contributed materials which promoted the establishment of well-defined and difficult techniques for the use of the arts. In our time, whenever art is propagated, the process has to start with art education. There was a long road to go between the foundation of the first 'Art and Trade School' in Quebec (seventeenth century) by Mgr. Laval and the initiation of the 'School of Fine Arts' in 1923 in Montreal. The creation of these schools was not the result of public action at large but, as it was always the same in Europe, of a small elected few. The period mentioned above embraces the growth of Canadian Art from the first tentative craftsmen up to its present state. The result of this development was the formation of two competing centres of artistic and literary life —Toronto and Montreal. It may be said that the 'official' history of painting in Canada starts with the works of Kane in Toronto and Krieghoff in Quebec.

This development takes two clearly different courses. We

find first a group of artists attracted by foreign art-schools, and rejecting the 'native' tradition of Canadian Art. The clearest example is supplied by the Scottish-Canadian James William Morrice (1865–1924) who developed cosmopolitan tendencies in his subjects as well as in his style. The second group comprises those who found fulfilment in painting Canadian landscapes and characters. Halfway between these two groups we find a number of artists—such as the 'Group of Seven' in Toronto, to be mentioned later—who painted the Canadian landscape but renewed its typical character by the application of so-called modern conceptions.

Apart from Krieghoff, already mentioned, O. R. Jacobi (1812–1901) also belongs to the period of early regional and topographical painting. Both painters are of German descent; their works show a certain measure of influence from the Dutch school of painting, but even so both artists have great individuality and personal style. The 'Canadian Autumn' of Jacobi shows a very smooth but expressive technique and an intimate appreciation of Nature which, however, will eventually pass through a Renaissance. Excellent interiors are painted by Paul Peel (1859–1892), and the finest example of his art, the 'Spinner', may be admired in the Museum of Fine Arts in Montreal. As the Church plays such an important role in Canadian life, it is understandable that many admirable religious paintings have been produced; of them we mention only the 'Saint Raphael' by Antoine Plamondon. Apart from painting, sculpture and architecture are responsible for several beautiful works of sacred art. Good examples of these are the hand-carved, painted statues, created in 1870, of St. Peter and St. Paul by Jean Baptiste Coté, in Quebec.

The most famous creator of secular monuments is Philippe Hebert (1850–1917). Aurel Suzor-Coté (1869–1937) belongs as a painter to the disciples of the Group of Seven in Toronto, but as a sculptor he has created many interesting smaller works of art. Early Church architecture is best represented by the Church of the Holy Family on Orleans Island and the one in the Ursuline Convent at Quebec, as well as by magnificent

Notre-Dame in Montreal. In modern times, inspired by the style and dimensions of St. Peter's in Rome, it is represented by St. James' Cathedral and by St. Joseph Shrine in Montreal. Not all of the older churches are entirely beautiful from the artistic point of view. The interior in particular, sometimes with an excess of plaster figures, frequently shows that often it was not only the artist who decided in all particulars on matters of construction.

Canadian cities were originally homely in construction, but this pleasant picture has suffered from a wave of Victorian architecture. It is fortunate that many of these ugly constructions are doomed to die in our time. Business centres tend to show skyscraper-construction, but the residential quarters of many cities have pleasant areas where modern architecture may be found at its best. Here beauty has blended well with efficiency.

The development of musical life in many Canadian cities, strongly influenced by new immigrants, during the last decades has been remarkable. Good orchestras provide an ever-growing public with classical music, and the number of opera performances has increased considerably. Apart from several noteworthy works of sacred music, Canada so far has not shown particular prominence in this field.

It is perhaps necessary to mention that the preceding pages are merely intended to convey an introduction for the better understanding of the following monographic studies. Its scope does not allow for more space to be used on a preface, nor has it been the intention to write a complete introduction to Canadian art and literature. Interested readers will find a reference-list on the subject at the end of the book. The author sincerely hopes that his work will contribute towards winning new friends for Canadian works of art and poetry.

I cannot close this preface without a word of thanks to my colleagues Mr. John L. Harrison (George Williams College, Montreal) and Mr. Macculoe (Cambridge, England). They have contributed to the formation of this book and Mr. Harrison, besides his help in poetry translation, has pointed out passages where alteration seemed necessary and often suggested how it might be made.

A. Chas v. Guttenberg

Joseph Marmette

The thunderstorms which affected the political and social atmosphere of Europe in the middle of the nineteenth century hardly penetrated to the shores of the St. Lawrence. Almost a hundred years had passed since the tempest of 1763 menaced the very existence of the French-Canadian settlers in Canada. The uprising of 1837 in Lower Canada was followed for a time by a policy of oppression of the French-Canadians.

Nevertheless the first symptoms of future mutual interests between the two big language-groups become soon evident in the political field and we find ourselves in the atmosphere favouring the forthcoming Canadian Confederation. Economically the colony is prosperous, and both groups seem to honour a silent understanding that it is desirable to prevent major mishaps to the growing harmony.

Owing to economic prosperity Quebec and Montreal became rich and elegant cities, and this situation of affluence affected neighbouring towns, which had already become fairly numerous. In all these cities, a level of civilisation had been reached which did not permit the rejection of artists and authors as inferior beings, of no particular use to society, and labelled with an expression of pity: 'So-and-so is no good, he just writes'. Nearly the opposite had now become fashionable. It was considered good manners to be able to talk about literature and art and even to use pen or brush personally, if one had sufficient money or spare time.

The little town of Montmagny is situated about thirty miles from Quebec on the south shore of the St. Lawrence River. In this town the rich physician Joseph Marmette senior married Elisa, a daughter of the highly-reputed family of Sir Etienne Pascal Taché. On the 25th of October 1844 a son, Joseph, was born. He was not a robust child, but rather graceful and fragile, with remarkable lively dark eyes. As a very young child he was said to be already most sensitive and endowed with a strong perception of right and wrong. He was not so much attracted by games and sports as by the books in his parents' library.

His imagination was fired by the works of Walter Scott and 'The Leatherstocking Tales' by Fenimore Cooper, a book which in Canada can still be considered very close to reality. In particular, he loved the saga and legends of his own country. When he was thirteen years old he became a boarder of the Quebec Gymnasium, where he completed his classical studies in 1864. He describes college life in his last unfinished autobiographical novel 'Going through Life' (A travers la vie), and it seems that this period of his life was not an experience of joy but rather of oppression; consequently he impatiently looked forward to its finish. In contrast with the college years of many other authors, Joseph was what one calls 'a good pupil'. The more light spirited amongst his friends admired the quiet poise which kept him from extremes. This characteristic he possibly owed in part to his inborn nature and in part to the social life of his parents' home which attracted many educated and cultured men and women.

By the end of his college period he showed such a strong preference for literature that all his friends were surprised to find him selecting the faculty of law at the University of Quebec. Actually this was not at all surprising, because the clever young man was anything but a Bohemian and doubtless had one eye on his future. Furthermore, the study of law would not mitigate his thirst for freedom and his already pronounced rejection of falseness in literary matters. He certainly had not been educated in the belief that the traditional rules of society need not be observed. His choice might be explained by a desire to refine his inborn feeling for 'right and fair' in his own life as well as in the lives of others, also making of the young Frenchman a typically correct English gentleman.

Marmette was born under a lucky star. His excellent personal qualities and the background of social standing of his parents were enhanced by the preference shown for him by Pierre Joseph Chauveau, at that time Prime Minister of the Province of Quebec, himself a poet and historian of distinction. The Minister offered the young attorney a position in the Ministry of Finance, which left him enough leisure to indulge his passion for reading. He showed a strong preference for the works of Balzac. The passion for reading probably produced his outstanding interest in the study of records, of which he found an abundance in the Ministries of Quebec. In 1867 he tried his hand in authorship and published his first short novel 'Charles and Eve' in the 'Revue Canadienne'. The same Review had been used in the previous year by Napoleon Bourassa for publishing his story 'James and Mary', which opened the series of French-Canadian historical novels.

The period for publications of this nature was well chosen, as in the year 1867 the status of Confederation was established, and this brought about the most important step towards national independence of the French-speaking group of citizens. The historical novel, therefore, may be appraised as a fresh blossoming of national pride, a sentiment justified by the heroic events of Canadian history. Would it be private interest which leads the employee of the Finance Ministry to use his leisure for reading provincial records and writing historical works? Or is it the influence of the most important national historian of Canada, François Xavier Garneau, who became his father-in-law? This historian, who understood so well how to portray the past of his country with the versatile pen of a Voltaire, the philosophic penetration of a Guizot and the vivacity of a Michelet, rests in the cemetery of Belmont, very near Quebec-city and adjoining the tragic battleground of Saint-Foy, of which he described the drama and glory with such perfection. Whenever Marmette, official and author, looked down from the castle on the cemetery, the poet in him must have been thrilled by the memory of this impressive spirit.

Be that as it may, with his first historical novel 'Charles and Eve', Marmette seems to have taken the providential road that he was to follow from now on. The story begins with the terrible massacre perpetrated by the Indians amongst the French colonists in 1689 in the little village of Lachine, located on the St. Lawrence near Montreal. It is recounted with great bitterness that the British settlers on the shore of the river instigated the Indians to this horrible action. The French noble De Montet, who had lost all his relatives amongst those who were murdered, decided to take revenge and marched with his small group of colonists and Hurons to New-England. Amongst them was a young French officer, Charles Dupuis, who plays an important role in the story. They progressed undetected over hidden trails to a spot near Schenectady, but here misfortune overtook them. Their presence was discovered by an Indian who had formerly lost his sweetheart during a battle with French settlers. He decided to use this favourable opportunity to take revenge, which was, however, to take some time, as will be seen presently.

The strategy of De Montet's little band was successful in so far that they reached the village undetected during the night. It was promptly attacked; all living creatures were mercilessly killed and all homes set afire. The last house still offering resistance is now besieged by Dupuis, his servant Fournier, and their ally the Huron chief 'Black Eagle'. At long last the house is taken and the attacking party finds a young girl, Eva Lorimier, a catholic French-woman, whose father had accepted the Protestant religion as a Huguenot. Dupuis experienced a furious love at first sight for the young girl, but so did the Indian chief Black Eagle, who wanted to carry her off to his wigwam. Their rivalry caused the strongest possible hate between the two men. All the defendants of the house were massacred, with the exception of the young girl who was to be taken to Quebec.

After this successful expedition of revenge it was decided to start on the march home, but the unsuspecting band was suddenly attacked by a strong troupe of hostile Indians. All seems lost. But the servant of Dupuis saves the day by making a bomb out of the remaining gunpowder and hurling it amongst the attacking party. The Indians, unaccustomed to such a terrible noise, flee but take Fournier with them as a prisoner. The victory therefore was on the French side, but now they found themselves in the midst of the Canadian winter without provisions and without gunpowder for hunting game.

The march continues, but it is evident that the band is being overcome by exhaustion; Black Eagle dies as a result of injuries sustained during the battle; Eve is exhausted to the point of death and can go no further. Despairing, Dupuis tries to hunt game and finally kills a reindeer, but he is too weak to cut up the animal. Fortunately Fournier, who had escaped from the Indians, arrives on the scene and helps Dupuis to transport the animal to the camp. This is salvation for the exhausted party, and from now on the march proceeds without mishap. They eventually arrive at Montreal, at this time called Ville Marie, and in June 1690 Charles and Eve are married.

This novel has many interesting features. The events related are based on historical facts. The same is true as regards the murderous horror which marks both white nationals in their own battles as well as against the Indians, evidence of the savage primitiveness of those times, widely different from the chivalrous usages which marked the battles of the European Baroque period. Apart from the historical value, it must be observed that the author gives rein to what Goethe called 'the desire for making fables'. The sequence of events takes place with the quickness and liveliness of a film, and the reader might at times think he is enjoying parts of the 'Count of Monte Cristo'. It is also evident that the language of the novel does not reach the level of Dumas.

The work, however, was well liked by the reading public. If it had been published in Europe, the chances are that it would have taken a place amongst adventure stories about the Indians. The European reader would not have been able to appreciate the peculiarly intangible atmosphere of the novel which is typically Canadian. This atmosphere is felt between the lines of the book as a memory of the nearly unbearable times in which the ancestors lived, and through the awareness that their early battles have been continued by their children to the point of victory. The novel, to the foreign reader only an adventure story, was seen by the French-Canadian as an old page of his family records. If you are not a Canadian, you will not perhaps be particularly touched by the portrayal of Nature provided by Marmette in the cinematographic relation of the events; when to explain the stress, for example, he simply writes: '. . . because it was winter', the foreign reader has no inkling of the significance of a Canadian winter.

It was only in 1870 that Marmette, after a most penetrating study of the records, provided his readers with his second novel 'François de Bienville'. This work surpasses his first novel in quantity of events, passions and catastrophes, and this is probably the reason why it is the best read—but not the best—book of this author. The period in which the story takes place is full of tension. The British had made the decision to attack the city of Quebec and Phipps was appointed as leader of the expedition. Against this background the story begins. A British officer, Harthing, meets a French-Canadian girl, Mary Louise d'Orcy, in Boston, where she lived in the home of her brother. He falls desperately in love with her. Marmette takes a full page to portray the attractions of this young lady and her extraordinary beauty. He also does some moralising by comparing this ideal, represented by Mary d'Orcy, with the unhealthy existence of many other girls of this period, who spend most of their lives in the ballrooms of the city.

Since this is a period in which French-speaking Canada as a whole refuses to become English, it is self-evident that the beautiful French-Canadian will refuse to marry the Britisher. The young man, humiliated by her refusal, decides to take revenge. He joins the band of Phipps as a volunteer, and having learned that the young girl had become a resident of Quebec, he succeeds, with the help of an Indian, in ascertaining her address. He commits the indiscretion of making his presence known to her by a letter, and not a message of love, but one full of threats. An attempt to kidnap the young beauty fails. Now the hero of the novel, Bienville, makes his appearance. He too loves Mary Louise, but with more chance of success than his rival. The British attack Quebec. Bienville kills Harthing during the battle, and the Indian who served Harthing inflicts serious wounds on Mary Louise's brother. Deep sisterly love and despair lead Miss d'Orcy to vow to enter a convent if Providence will cure her brother.

This actually happens and Mary Louise renounces Bienville. With a broken heart Bienville returns to Montreal and seeks his death in battle against the Iroquois. Just before a big attack on an Iroquois camp, he receives a letter from Quebec informing him that the Bishop is inclined to release Mary Louise of her vows. Bienville touches the heights of earthly happiness, but fate is against him. The attack on the Iroquois starts and in the course of the battle Bienville suddenly comes face to face with the Indian previously employed by Harthing. The two men attack each other ferociously and finally the Indian is vanquished but not before fatally wounding Bienville.

The success of the second book served as a strong incentive to the author, and his third work appeared in 1872. It is certainly not inferior to the previous novels as regards vivacity and historical interest, and psychologically it reflects the greater experience and maturity of the author. 'Intendant Bigot' was a very sinister historical personality of the later years of French sovereignty. There was 'something rotten' in this state of French administration, and the background of the book portrays the dark fate approaching the French colonists. The Britishers advance and Bigot, a sensual brute, acts as traitor. Around this primitive adventure Marmette forges a chain of too numerous events, which somewhat spoils the effect of the impressive historical background of the book. Canadian critics have expressed the opinion that Bigot was painted in colours much too dark. On the other hand, Bigot being a traitor, seems to have deserved the picture; Marmette at any rate found it adequate.

After this slight adversity Marmette reached the top of his career with his novel 'Chevalier de Mornac'. This book deals with a problem of immigration. Small, elegant, self-contained and clever, Marmette, by this time a well-established official, perhaps did not too much like many of his more robust compatriots. Reading the novel carefully, one gets the impression that it was written on impulse, Marmette desiring numerous French cavaliers as his rural compatriots. The book seems to a great extent to have been written as a justification of this desire. It is clear enough that Mornac from Gascogne serves as an example of the French nobleman, and, as a type, we know him fairly well from the period of the 'Song of Roland' right up to Dumas. This is how Marmette portrays Mornac, who disembarks from his vessel in Quebec; 'Notwithstanding his somewhat shabby apparel, our knight looked noble and bold. He was tall, tanned and his long aristocratic face indicated an age of about twenty-eight years. His nose had the shape of the beak of an eagle and he had a heavy black moustache of which the points were carefully twirled around the corners of his strong, ironical mouth. Only the warriors of Richelieu's time had such beautiful moustaches, which gave a man such a self-conscious look and which were so loved by the ladies. . . . And his black intelligent eyes looking upward, his gaze wandered over the Cape of Diamonds: By Jove! So this is the poor small Capital where we intend to court Dame Fortune!'

Throughout the book, Mornac distinguishes himself clearly and continuously from the multitude of those who appear in the story. In an unmistakable way he stands apart; his bearing and thoughts throughout the events are quite different from those of the peasants, traders and trappers. He is, and he always remains, the ideal picture of a cavalier, and this is only to be expected since he had to be an example. If on one hand it may be considered as a weakness of the novel, on the other it gives Marmette the opportunity of portraying his knight

27

with all the qualities of perfection; he never attained it again in the personalities of his novels. It almost seems as if he had given shape to a long cherished and secret drama of his life.

Marmette portrays in his novels, with a high degree of truth, all the horrors of colonial life and war, and apart from this he consciously or unconsciously points the way towards a more human and refined civilisation, as represented in some of his personalities and examples. Of these personalities Mornac is the most perfect. Perhaps his last work may be considered as one of the least obtrusive educational novels. We know that all the people who met Marmette personally had a sincere esteem for him. This is easily explained by his fine character and the attraction of his gentleness and sincere desire to help. If Marmette had lived two hundred years before, there is no doubt that he would have behaved exactly as the Chevalier de Mornac.

The condensed story is easily told. In full, however, with its abundance of events, it cannot be rendered easily: one has to read it. In the city of Quebec, a small town at that time, Mornac finds his lovely cousin, Miss Richecourt, and promptly falls in love with her. Peculiar personalities move in the milieu of the small colonial town. Another pretender to the heart of Miss Richecourt is Vilarme, notwithstanding the fact that this man murdered the girl's mother in France. And finally we have a good-natured but insignificant young man, Jolliet, who is also keen to marry the young beauty. One day these three people travel together towards a small village on the St. Lawrence, to help with harvesting. An Indian by the poetic name of Bear's Paw believes he has reason to wreak revenge on Mornac, and with a band of Iroquois he attacks the party. All are taken prisoner and transported towards the north where the Indians have their camp on the Hudson River. The horrible savagery of these Indians is portrayed in great detail in the description of the voyage. After arrival in the Indian camp we have every opportunity to admire the strategy, the cold-blooded courage and the humour of the cavalier, never daunted by the most serious situations. Mornac

succeeds in making use of the time-honoured means of the
white race to overcome the Indians; with the help of a barrel
of 'fire-water' he makes them all drunk. It ought to be remembered that the Iroquois, as a tribe, received their pay from the
English. Meanwhile a group of Mornac's friends from Quebec
together with the Huron chief Black Fox, had opened a search
for the missing party and had arrived in the neighbourhood of
the Indian camp. The Hurons were friends of the French, in
part because these gave them certain advantages, in part
because it is characteristic of the Indians never to lose an
opportunity to destroy each other. This historical truth ought
to be remembered by those who think that the savages were a
better type of men than their so called white oppressors.

Black Fox penetrates the Iroquois camp and murders as
many of his drunken enemies as he can. In self-protection
Mornac has to kill Vilarme and saves Miss Richecourt. After
many adventures the survivors of the party return to Quebec.
Mornac, however, is not at all daunted by the dangers he has
braved. He joins an expedition to rebuild the burned-out Fort
Richelieu, which protects the trade-routes against the menace
of the Indians. The Indians, however, become aware of these
plans. A battle results and Mornac finds himself face to face
with his old hateful enemy, the Iroquois Bear's Paw. The
Indian is taken a prisoner and, in accordance with existing
war-custom, is burned at the stake. The expedition progresses
triumphantly; later on the party returns to Quebec and
Mornac marries Miss Richecourt.

The author shows further advance in his art in his novel
'The Fiancée of the Rebel', published in 1875 in the Revue
Canadienne. The action of this dramatic story is very exciting,
but less loaded with barbarism. More important still, the
language is much more accomplished than before. Again, this
novels but short stories, or—as the one called 'Gigot and his
the city of Quebec in the year 1774, a time of poisonous
antagonism between Britishers and Frenchmen. The basis of
the book is a love story, with political interests. The fiancée,
Alice Cognard, receives fervent attentions from both a

French-Canadian and a Britisher; in the battle of jealousy between the two men, the political and military history of that period is revealed. As in the epic poem of the Nibelungen, love ends in tragedy and it is only the stillness of death that ends both love and hate.

It is a fair question to ask why Marmette always presents in his novels an historical background, even for tales of love and the domestic life of woman. The explanation is that even a superficial study of available records of New France will show that the battle of the French-Canadians to obtain their autonomy, was fought not essentially by interested generals and a disinterested population, but by family against family and individual against individual. It was not only 'a man's war', we find that women too, throw themselves into the battle body and soul, more often than not properly armed for the purpose.

Every war, and not only this one, means (as we are continually being told with empty pathos) both the marching on and the heroic battles with enemy troops, and the honour, most doubtful in God's eyes, of killing as many human beings (supposed enemies) as possible. We should have sufficient insight to realise that war is nothing but the terrible always-returning conflict between Cain and Abel, which deeply penetrates all family and private affairs, and destroys what love has built. War deeply influences all human relations, just as all these relations dye the purpose of war, and an author successfully portrays nature if he fully reflects undivided life, and neglects no part of reality. The real significance of the battle for home and family, for the language and religion of the French-Canadian, becomes much clearer to us from the pages of Marmette's historical novels than from the total of military records kept in the archives.

Two years later, in 1877, Marmette published his novel 'Tomahawk and Sword'. This work, consisting of two parts, gave a new version of the historical events he had already portrayed in his previous novels, 'Chevalier de Mornac' and 'François de Bienville', and in particular of the siege of Quebec by the Britishers. One year later, in 1878, he published two other novels. The first 'Heroism and Treason', portrays in its first part the historical epic of Madelaine de Verchères, and in the second part (Traitors and Heroes) the period of the last years of French domination. Another new novel, 'The Macchabean of New-France' is of particular interest in that it makes us intimate with the family history of the Le Moyne's, whose members are often prominent in this period.

The most important event in the life of the author was his appointment in the year 1879 as Deputy High Commissioner of the Canadian Government in Paris, in which city he remained for nearly four years. With Marmette's personal qualities it stands to reason that he made many interesting acquaintances and real friends amongst the important authors and scientists prominent in the literary salons of that days. Of these, Anatole France and the historian Augustin Thierry deserve special mention. He developed a particular friendship with Maquet, the collaborator in the 'novel-factory' of Dumas. Later on this led to the slightly depreciatory nickname 'Marmette, the Dumas of Canada'. However, there is no necessity to defend Marmette against the opinion that he is nothing but an author of entertainment literature; his national importance for the French-Canadians has become very evident.

Paris provided Marmette with the final perfection of his literary and human personality, apart from the value of the friendships he made. Although not everyone might have seen it clearly, the man who returned to Canada in 1883 was a larger person than before. The Canadian poet Louis Frechette, who had known Marmette already from Quebec and was with him in Paris, expressed his admiration frankly and without jealousy: 'An invariable decency marks all his acts . . . ; his simple affirmation or promise was of greater value than the signatures of all Rothschilds of Europe and America. What passionate inclinations towards all ideals, all poetry, for all things beyond the routine of everyday life.'

Eventually Marmette became an important and esteemed

official of the Ottawa Government and held the position of Deputy Director of Records in Canada. Laval University in Quebec made him doctor honoris causa and the Royal Society elected him as a member. It is not surprising that the number of his friends, real and mercenary, increased considerably. He belonged to the 'Literary Circle of Ten', which at that time comprised the most important authors and poets of the country. Foreign guests liked to visit the elegant small man with the energetic face and the dark brilliant eyes. All these distinctions at the same time honoured his dearly-loved Fatherland in which—to contradict the platitude—he was allowed to be a prophet.

There was yet another valuable present which he brought home from France. Possibly out of regard for his subject-matter and the desired large readership for his books, he had formerly used a literary diction somewhat patriarchal in character. Compared with contemporary French novels his language often makes a somewhat heavy impression. After his return all this was a thing of the past. His writing from that time on was elegant and modern. We leave it to critics and readers to decide which of the two styles best represents the real atmosphere of the period.

In the next years Marmette made several voyages to Florida, England and France. After letting his pen rest for a short period, he published 'Stories and Memories' in 1891. In accordance with the title, these are not lengthy historical novels but short stories, or—as the one called 'Gigot and his Court'—repetitions of his historical novels with a stronger historical background. It is remarkable that the autobiographical character of his works and his own personal memories now became prominent. Was it possible that the fragile sickly man could already have heard the call of the Dark Angel which was to take him away in four years' time?

In 1895 Marmette started his autobiographical novel 'Straight through Life', and it was printed the same year. It will stand comparison with Goethe's 'Dichtung and Wahrheit —Fiction and Truth'. Real life and fantasies are mixed in the fate of Lucien Rambaud, the hero of the novel. It is a story of a dreamy youth with an eagerness for reading and a liking for writing poetry, impatiently awaiting the end of college life; he is a passionate patriot full of the joy of life and already touched by the sadness of disappointments which love has prepared for him. It is not a historical theme which forms the background of this novel. The action takes place in the period of Confederation, but the political background is not important compared with intimate personal experiences. The literary importance of the work lies in its provision of a colourful and most truthful expression of Canadian life. Fate did not allow the completion of the third part of the work, which was meant to be a trilogy. He died suddenly on the 7th of May 1895. His friend, Louis Frechette, took it upon himself to finish the third part of the scheme, making use of notes which Marmette had left behind.

A fair estimate of the value of Marmette's art has been provided by this congenial friend: 'Marmette had the temperament and Fancy of a powerful novelist of a good school. This implies that he knew how to tell a story well and did not belong to the school of vivisection of the soul, which only tries to analyse the intangible and fleeting impressions of the mind. . . . He is the real creator of the Canadian novel'.

William Kirby

Above the main door of the Quebec Post Office there is a
tablet portraying a dog gnawing a bone, and a date, 1736,
which accompanies the French version of the following lines:

> 'I am a dog that gnaws a bone
> I crouch and gnaw it all alone.
> A time will come which is not yet
> When I'll bite him by whom I'm bit.'

This tablet was erected on its present site by the merchant
Nicholas Jaquin dit Philibert when he set up a warehouse in
the Buade-Street. The 'Chien d'or' was to mark his opposition
to the monopoly of imports and exports imposed on the people
of New-France by the unscrupulous Royal Intendant, François
Bigot, the representative of Louis XV. From the 'Chien d'or'
William Kirby took the title of his novel 'The Golden Dog',
which was first published in 1877.

The action of the novel takes place in the troubled year
1748, at a time when England and France and their colonies
in the North-American continent were engaged in a war
which formed the prelude to the conquest of the French
colonies by the English in the Seven Years' War. By the treaty
which ended the previous war in 1713, France has lost her
title to Newfoundland, but had retained New-Brunswick. She
had built the port of Louisbourg on Cape Breton in the hope
of one day recapturing all of her colony of Acadia. Misunder-
standings about the line of the new frontier inflamed the
antagonisms of nationality, creed and language which divided
the two groups of colonies. The English were in firm posses-

34

sion of Hudson Bay and the English Hudson's Bay company competed with the French for the rich prize of the fur trade.

The French fur trade depended on friendship with the Huron and Algonquin Indians, traditional enemies of the Five Nations of the Iroquois who were supported by the English. Both sides sought allies among the Indians to further their commercial interests and this conflict added an independent and local cause to the many which made England and France enemies in Europe.

To the West Jolliet and La Salle had explored the Mississippi for France and set up a chain of forts from Lake Michigan to Louisiana which outflanked the New England colonies and held in the Iroquois. Against this thin barrier protecting French hopes of exploiting the unknown interior there surged the full force of the New Englanders' desire to settle an expanding population in new farm lands. The New Englanders wished to farm, the French to trade with the Indians. Ultimately the superior numbers of the New Englanders made them dominant, and France lost the opportunity of winning half a continent.

The early Intendants and Governors of New France, men of the purposeful character of Talon and Frontenac, had been inspired to enlarge their King's dominions. Louis XIV (1643–1715) and his forceful Minister, Colbert, had firmly supported their efforts until the preparation, conduct and consequences of war in Europe pre-occupied them. Louis XV (1715–1774), while insisting on maintaining a minute control over all the affairs of the colonies, was neglectful and vacillating in his policy towards them. He preferred feasts and voluptuous life to majesty and conscientious government. Aided immigration ended, and between 1723 and 1740 only 761 poachers, smugglers and petty offenders were brought to Canada, while the New England colonies became increasingly stronger in population and in wealth. Bigot used his office as Intendant for his own ends, but there remained some men in New France with faith and fortitude.

In the very year 1748 La Verendrye and his sons were

searching the Saskatchewan River for the fabled route to the
Western Sea which had successively attracted Cabot, Cartier,
and Champlain. In 1744, however, war had begun in Europe
and the French were given their opportunity to recapture their
territory and dispose of the New Englanders. They set out
from Louisbourg for Annapolis, the former French town of
Port Royal, but failed to take it. Louisbourg was in turn
attacked and occupied by the English. Both sides planned
expeditions which were either abandoned or ineffective, but
New France and Quebec were threatened.

The story has for its background this struggle of the powers
of the Old World for final supremacy in the New, and begins
with the work performed on the fortifications of Quebec,
which was then a small town of about 7,000 inhabitants. It
formed one end of the ribbon of settlements which struggled
thinly along the banks of the St. Lawrence through Three
Rivers to Montreal. Half of Quebec's inhabitants lived in the
cramped, irregular streets of the Lower Town, around the
church of Notre-Dame des Victoires, in a huddle as disorderly
and as French as the quais of Paris or Rouen. On the tall
cliffs which front Cape Diamond, the Upper Town stretched
from the redoubt where the Citadel was later built to the
banks of the St. Charles River where the Intendant had his
Palace. Within the fortification which defended the promon-
tory of Cape Diamond were the Cathedral, the Hotel Dieu,
the Governor's Château St. Louis, the Recollets, the Convent
of the Ursulines and all the buildings of Church and State
from which the Royal Province of New France was adminis-
tered. Outside the walls were newer suburbs, and, at some
distance, the Intendant's Château, Beaumanoir, whose ruins
can still be seen.

The reader is quickly introduced to the main persons of the
story, most of whom actually lived. Historians have corrected
some of the portraits, but an historian cannot replace a
novelist's insight into human character. François Bigot, the
Intendant, rules with subtle cunning the Grand Company of
Traders in New France, which was known to the people it

compulsorily plundered as 'la Friponne—the cheat'. Round him have collected all the dissolute and depraved drunkards, swaggerers and self-seekers of the country. During the day they abuse their official positions to amass fortunes which they spend at night with unrestrained profligacy in continued orgies. Kirby shows that, corrupt as Bigot is, he has qualities of fearlessness, occasionally of tenderness, and even of patriotism which make him mere credible in the story than he appears to have been in life. Bigot is purposefully and guilefully courteous and winning. He has been able to deprive Bourgeois Philibert of his estates in France, and the enmity between them has continued in New France where Philibert the honest merchant, has become rich. As leader of the 'honnêtes gens', the good people of the town, the Merchant of the Golden Dog is a threat to Bigot's sharp practices. These two represent the opposed forces which struggle for commercial power and political influence. The complicated relationships between the persons of the story which arise from the struggle make the intricate plot effective.

Philibert's son, Pierre, young manly and forthright, has returned from the fighting in Acadia. He nourishes an undeclared love for Amelia de Repentigny, his childhood friend who is similarly in love with him. He is able, by the influence for good which he has over her brother, Le Gardeur de Repentigny, to withdraw him from the degrading company of Bigot's associates. Bigot sees in Le Gardeur a means to ruin Bourgeois Philibert, the one appealing to the foolish imprudence of pleasure-loving youth, the other to the good-natured affection of a beloved friend and brother.

Le Gardeur is a conventional figure, but credible enough. The modern reader, however, may find it difficult to accept Amelia as anything more than a Sunday-School heroine. Vice as the detective-story writers well know, is more interesting than virtue, and virtuous love is the most difficult of subjects for a novelist. In the passages of the novel which deal with Amelia's love for Pierre Philibert, Kirby is at his most dated and least convincing. Amelia is one of those maidenly innocents who shed tears which are either bitter or suffused with joy, whose exquisite form has only lissom movements, whose cheek glows or crimsons, whose bosom is agitated, whose feet are dainty and ankles trim, whose countenance is radiant and whose voice tinkles with continual silvery laughter. Her most womanly quality is curiosity, her most feminine a quite genteel perversity, yet, even here, Kirby may provoke a response from the reader: 'The world is ruled by such dreams, dreams of impassioned hearts and improvisations of warm lips, not by cold words linked in chains of iron sequence—by love, not by logic. The heart with its passions, not the understanding with its reasoning, sways in the long run the actions of mankind.'

The strongest hold which Bigot's party has on Le Gardeur is through his overwhelming love for Angelique des Meloises: 'She was a woman keenly alive to admiration—jealous and exacting of her suitors, never willingly letting one loose from her bonds, and with warm passions and a cold heart was eager for the semblance of love, although never feeling its divine realty'. A deeply unhappy woman, she refuses to marry Le Gardeur; her ambition is to become the Intendant's Lady, as a step towards the Royal bed itself. Bigot is attracted by her undoubted beauty but cannot marry her for fear of displeasing his patroness, La Pompadour, the mistress of Louis XV. At the same time, he is sheltering at Beaumanoir, Caroline de St. Castin, a noble lady from Acadia, who, heartstricken at his desertion of her, but still infatuated with his considerable charm, has secretly left her father's home and followed him.

Kirby is much more successful with the characterisation of these two men, the one proud, unrepentant, scheming, yet aware of the strength of her desires and the frailty of her hopes, the other discouraged, defeated, subdued yet passionately loyal to a man she cannot fully trust.

Angelique fears the influence Caroline has on Bigot, and she discovers that he intends to keep the mysterious woman. A means to rid herself of her rival presents itself insistently to Angelique's mind: 'Angelique was playing a game of chess with Satan for her soul and felt that she was losing it'. She resolves to have Caroline murdered and engages La Corriveau, a witch-like woman, who is able to gain Caroline's confidence. La Corriveau kills Caroline with a poison in a secret room at Beaumanoir. In vicious spite, however, she stabs the body and thus Bigot discovers the murder and suspects Angelique of it. Angelique now knows she has lost her chance of marrying Bigot. Since the king has commanded a search for Caroline, Bigot cannot reveal his knowledge. He buries the body secretly, and, though full of remorse, determines to turn the attention of the searchers by a grand blow at Bourgeois Philibert. He promises Angelique to his secretary, de Pean, if he can contrive the death of Bourgeois Philibert.

De Pean plans to goad Le Gardeur into killing Bourgeois. Pierre Philibert, in spite of his betrothal to Amelia, Le Gardeur's sister, is then likely to revenge himself on Le Gardeur and the 'Friponne' would be left supreme. Le Gardeur is incensed at the loss of Angelique, and de Pean finds it easy to madden him further with drink and bring him to the Market Place where a crowd has gathered to hear a sermon. A suitable incident is arranged, and Le Gardeur, urged by Angelique, at an imagined insult from Bourgeois Philibert, unknowingly kills him. Overcome by his crime, he surrenders to the Guard. Pierre does not attempt revenge: he forgives Le Gardeur. Amelia in deep sorrow enters the Convent of the Ursulines, declines and dies.

In Europe the war has ended with the Peace of Aix-la-Chapelle, and the story closes with a brief account of the fate of its persons. Bigot and the 'Friponne' prosper till their mismanagement allows New France to fall to the English in the Seven Years' War. Le Gardeur sent by the King's command to France, is eventually freed without trial and dies after a dedicated military life in India. Pierre resumes his soldiering. Angelique marries de Pean and flourishes. La Corriveau is convicted of another crime and gibbeted at Nevis: 'Our tale is now done. There is in it neither poetic nor human justice.'

That is perhaps its chief merit: it is close to history. The murder of Philibert was an actual event. The murderer escaped but was pursued by Philibert's son and killed in India. The house of Angelique des Meloises where Montcalm later died, can still be seen, and the flame lit in the Ursuline Chapel by a Madelaine de Repentigny in 1719 burns still. Another Repentigny was for a time Mayor of Quebec, and a small village outside the city is called by the same name. Caroline de St. Castin existed at least in legend which holds that she died violently in mysterious circumstances. Kirby uses his material freely to make a satisfying story, but he does not distort events or persons of any importance to do so.

His knowledge of the period is scholarly and thorough and he gives an exact picture of the life of the time, much of it based on the writings of Mr. Kalm who appears in the novel and who said at the time, 'I have found that eminent persons, generally speaking, in this country, have much more taste for natural history and literature than in the English colonies, where the majority of people are engrossed in making their fortune, while science is as a rule held in very light esteem'. Kirby shows the reader the polite society of the aristocracy in Quebec, its balls, dinners and amusements, its intrigues, flirtations, gossip and frivolities, the gay activities of the regiments of the 'Roussillon' and 'Beard', and the work of the Church in hospital, convent and seminary, in converting the Indians, in protecting them from unscrupulous traders who wished to sell them 'fire-water', and in making alliances with them against hostile tribes and the English. The life of the habitants on the estates is not forgotten. Contemporary customs are faithfully described. One of these was the May Day ceremony. The 'censitaires' or dependants of the 'Seigneur' set up a tall fire-tree stripped of its bark in front of the Manor House. After traditional dancing, shots were fired at the tree till it was thoroughly blackened. It was then the turn of the 'Seigneur' to acknowledge the mutual loyalty of master and servant. He gave a large and prolonged feast to all his dependants.

Kirby presents the life of the countryside in the days of the Seigneurial system idyllically, and in so doing is substantially correct. The system was not as harsh as the feudal one in France from which it derived. The different conditions of a new country led to advantageous modifications. The Seigneur had certain judicial powers and rights of fishing and hunting, but Seigneuries could be bought so that some noble families were reduced to peasant status and many peasants became proprietors. As far as we can judge it was a harmonious society, but Kirby neglects to show that handicapped by lack of capital and overridden by the Court of Versailles, the French colonies were unable to make the same material progress as those of New England. At this time the New England colonies were beginning to develop a culture independent of their origins, but New France was still dominated by Paris and Versailles.

No Englishman appears in the novel and the clash of the two nations is presented in military terms only. This may lead the readers to suspect that Kirby's interest in the period is merely antiquarian, and that 'The Golden Dog' is a conventional novel in the accepted literary tradition of Kirby's time. It cannot be described as purely Canadian, though Kirby himself was a great nationalist. The ludicrous figure of the itinerant notary, Jean Pothier dit Robin, and the other warmly conceived characters of humble station, beggars, ferrymen, singers and servants, owe something to Scott, and perhaps to John Galt, the novelist of Scottish life who lived for a time in Canada. Indeed, there is a general and inevitable debt to European writers like Scott and Dumas, and an indirect one to the American, Fenimore Cooper, from whom John Richardson has taken the impetus to establish the historical novel in Canada before Kirby wrote 'The Golden Dog'. The influence of the 'Gothic' novelists may be seen in the horrific portrait of La Corriveau and in the apparatus of secret tunnels, hidden rooms, poisoned flowers and mysterious letters which helps the story along. The touch of the macabre, slight as it is in Kirby, comes mainly from the earliest English writers 'Monk' Lewis and Radcliffe, whose dark melodramas were widely read, although Edgar Allan Poe had re-created this type of writing in a fashion appropriate to the change of time and place.

Kirby has perhaps been eclipsed by the wider fame of Sir Gilbert Parker who followed him, but the opinion of Sir John George Bourinot, an Honorary Secretary of the Royal Society of Canada, is representative of Kirby's contemporaries: 'There is one respect in which Canadians have never won any marked success, and that is in the novel or romance. With the single exception of The Golden Dog . . . I cannot point to one which shows much imaginative or literary skill.' The novel was first published in 1877, and has run to seven Canadian editions, including one since the war. There have been many pirated American editions, an indication of its popularity. It has twice been translated into French, and has been published in London. Thus it has maintained the place given to it by its first tremendous, and, at that time, unprecedented appeal.

To the reader in our time parts of 'The Golden Dog' may be tedious, but that is a measure of the change in popular taste. The length of the novel may be forbidding, but it contains some vigorous writing and a creditable handling of contrasted incidents. The Plot is less contrived than might be expected from the date it was written. Indeed Kirby, like some modern novelists, selects a situation and explores it thoroughly. At times he is irritatingly learned and eager to parade that knowledge of quotations, authors, languages, and events which betrays the writer who has no original force and is dependent on the support of others to maintain supremacy over the reader. Though his manner of writing is often second-hand, it remains competent and concise, and though the novel has less value now than when it was written it is still worth attention. Kirby may not succeed in creating a genuine Canadian mode of thought and feeling, for he was born an Englishman, but he was aware of the need to do so. Behind this picture of Canada in the days of the French there is an earnest but unobtrusive hope that the twin traditions of France and England would coalesce: 'Then the two glorious streams of modern thought and literature united in New France where they ran side by side to this day—in time to be united in one grand flood stream of Canadian literature.'

Kirby himself by his sympathetic interest in a people and a history at first alien to him contributed to this progress. The story of his life is symbolic of the fusions from which Canada today draws her strength. He was born in 1817 at Kingston-upon-Hull, England, and bore a thoroughly Yorkshire name. In 1832 he came with his parents to Canada. He was educated at Cincinnati, Ohio, and settled in Niagara where he married, and edited and published the 'Mail' for twenty years. From 1871 to 1895 he occupied the post of Collector of Customs at Niagara, where he died in 1906.

His first publication was a 'Counter-Manifesto to the Annexationists of Montreal' in 1849, in which he opposed the extreme Tory merchants of Montreal who, fearful of the political power given to the French by the Rebellion Losses Bill and disappointed by the British policy of Free Trade, wished to join the United States. Throughout his life Kirby remained a firm United Empire Loyalist and he was called on to address the Centennial which they held at Niagara in 1884. His long poem of twelve cantos, 'The U.E.' of 1859 tells the story of the founders of Niagara and deals with the Rebellion of 1837, when the 'Fils de la Liberté' under Papineau allied themselves with the Radicals of Upper Canada to demand a measure of responsible government. Although the rising was crushed by force it drew British attention to discontent in the colonies and was the occasion of Lord Durham's famous Report.

Kirby's poetry is pedestrian and derivative and it nowhere equals the merit of his novel. He continued the Loyalist-tradition in poetry, following Oliver Goldsmith (1781–1861), the namesake and relative of the Irish poet. Kirby also wrote fourteen sonnets including a National song 'Canadians for Ever'. For the most part they are competent but uninspired echoes of Pope and Milton, very much following a tradition which had died in England at the beginning of the nineteenth century. In addition, as can be told from 'The Golden Dog', he was greatly interested in Canadian history. He wrote on

Pontiac, Bushy Run and published his 'Annals of Niagara' in 1896. As a Loyalist he had political interests and helped to write a lector's companion in support of his local party.

This close identification with his adopted country, his work as a newspaper editor and local historian, and his contribution to Canadian literature made him a fitting founder-member of the Royal Society of Canada, which was instituted in the year 1882 in the circumstances thus related by Bourinot: '. . . while this Confederation is fighting its way out of its political difficulties and resolving wealth and refinement from the original and ragged elements of a new country, it is for the respective nationalities not to stand aloof from one another, but to unite in every way possible for common intellectual improvement, and give sympathetic encouragement to the study of the two languages and to the mental efforts of each other'.

William Kirby became Vice President of the English Literature Section of the Royal Society and helped to further the unification of the country for which he had so much and spontaneous feeling: 'Eternity would be too short to weary one of this lovely scene—this bright Canadian morning is worthy of Eden and the glorious landscape worthy of such a sunrising'.

Octave Crémazie

The influence of a poet on posterity originates in the works he leaves behind him, but is not limited to these. To mention only one example, we find that the tragic personality of Dante is just as important to us as the tragedy he wrote. Often it is the heroic or patriotic attitude of a poet that is an incentive for later generations. Octave Crémazie belongs to this group.

He was born on the 16th of April 1827, in the old city of Quebec, with its crooked streets and cobbled ways to the upper town, the most European and French city of the American continent. He was the son of a retired merchant; his childhood was happy, he had two brothers, his parents loved him dearly, and there were no worries. But the boy, who entered the historically famous Quebec seminary, failed to distinguish himself as brilliant; the development of his personality in the directions for which he was to become noted had not yet begun. It was his teacher, the Abbé Holmes, who through the influence he gained over the lad first disclosed the future pattern. Professor Holmes was one of those fully developed personalities who dedicate a lifetime to the cultivation of the mind; he was a classic example of this type and an exemplary guide for the young men under him.

Young Octave must have been similarly disposed, else the leaping spark would not so quickly have been blown to a flame. From the moment of meeting onwards, the Jesuit Abbé Holmes was not only his teacher but also his best friend, one who gradually opened to him one spiritual room after another, each one filled with the riches of past thought. The young man rapidly developed a great hunger for learning, and was

45

assisted by an excellent memory. This is the explanation of the
fact that Octave Crémazie was not only a master of French,
Latin and Greek literature, but—following the example of his
teacher—was also at home in the Spanish, German, English
and Scandinavian languages. He even knew Arabian and
Sanskrit literature. Hearing of such a feat of learning with a
measure of surprise, we moderns might offer the criticism that
such a mental discipline must have drawn unduly upon the
time and energy which should have been devoted to the
Natural Sciences, quite apart from such profane pursuits as an
understanding of book-keeping and business management. If
one has not chosen the career of a lecturer, the lack of such
knowledge in his milieu and time might easily lead to disaster
—which actually happened in the case of Crémazie, as we
shall see later.

Obviously the good Abbé could not foresee that the humanistic studies pursued by the young man without any counter-
weight would produce a demon—in the sense of the great
Greek philosopher Socrates—that would take a stranglehold
on his soul. It seemed that everything else had lost its savour
for the youth, in comparison with the urge that directed his
whole existence. After finishing college, the quite common
problem of selecting a profession had to be solved. Old Jacques
Crémazie was quite able to afford a good education for his
three boys, but it was such a drain on his resources that he felt
somewhat pressed to put his children in a position where they
could look after themselves. Octave's two older brothers,
Jacques and Joseph, fortunately had not carried their eagerness for knowledge to the point of losing touch with practical
life. More realistic than Octave, one became a lawyer and a
professor of civil law at the University of Quebec, and the
other a notary. Apart from this, and in good American style,
the two brothers had founded a small bookshop, a source of
income which became fairly promising in connection with the
eager, newly-born intellectual life of the city.

It seemed a very natural solution that Octave should join
them as a partner and collaborator in the venture, and that he

should soon become the real manager of the business, as his two brothers had much to do in their own profession. The first address of the 'Librairie Crémazie' was at a modest and not very bright room in Bleury Street, which descended from the centre of town to the then military port. Although it was fairly remote from the centre of the town, business went well from the start, and the gratifying revenue of the shop was proof of the business ability of the elder brothers. The formation and development of the business took place in part during a feverish period of growing intellectual interests, prior to the literary renaissance of 1860 and the political triumph of 1867. After a long period of mental stagnation the new hopes of national liberty worked as an incentive in all fields of endeavour. The beginning of a new and favourable economic era also contributed towards a general feeling of coming improvement. The cultivated spirits amongst the population, who had suffered most from the oppression, reacted with a sudden blossoming of patriotic art and literature. It is easily understood that the hunger for mental nourishment, particularly for books imported from Paris, rapidly grew.

It is not surprising, on the contrary it is easy to understand that Octave Crémazie credited himself and his business abilities for a good part of the financial success of their venture. He was uncritical with regard to himself and carried away in the stream of these moving times, and the fact that he had an exaggerated conception of his business abilities certainly contributed to the financial catastrophe awaiting him in the future.

Actually he was anything but a businessman. Perhaps he could have been one if his education had been different: we do not know. One thing is certain: the very strong accent on his humanistic training had left no room for real business sense, and had in fact created a certain disdain for money and money matters. It would frequently happen that he would forget to cash cheques and attend to other rudimentary but essential business details, when puzzling out the meaning of a poem. Accountancy—that indispensable safeguard of every

47

business—remained under his supervision in a state best described as elementary. Notwithstanding all this, thanks to favourable external influences the business progressed to the point where it was necessary to consider moving to the centre of town and finding larger accommodation. So in 1855 we discover the 'Librairie Crémazie' settled in the Rue de la Fabrique, always full of traffic, in a shop which had large show-windows on the street, and with an excellent stock of literature. A large number of curious people as well as actual purchasers could always be found looking at the attractive display of the latest products of recently-imported French literature.

In a back-room of the shop, Octave had his sanctum, to which only his inner circle of friends, poets, authors, professors and politicians was admitted. In this room filled to capacity with books of all descriptions in accordance with Crémazie's taste, the remaining space almost completely blocked by small tables loaded with vases and bric-à-brac, he could be found for the greater part of the day at his desk, equally covered with all kinds of objects. There he could be found perhaps glancing through some new edition, his visitors all around engaged in lively discussions, using as seats anything not completely covered with the pieces of his collections.

Physically, Octave was not an Adonis. His body was small and thick-set like a sailor's; it was possibly an inheritance from his Breton ancestors, on his mother's side. A glance at his broad, pleasant face, his near-sighted eyes behind strong glasses, his bald head, suggested rather a well-to-do dry goods merchant, and certainly did not reveal the highly-developed mind of its owner.

Yet Octave Crémazie was a typical representative of the intellectual of his time, and such a powerful force in the cultural life of his home city, long before he wrote important poetry and quite apart from the attraction of his bookshop. He was the centre for all who had inscribed on their banner the cause of the intellectual and national progress of French-Canadian citizenship. Consequently, important authors and politicians met in his room, amongst them Abbé Ferland, Abbé Casgrain, the future minister Chauveau, the French Consul Baron Gauldrée-Boileau, the historian Alfred Garneau, the poets Frechette and Lemay, and many others. Here was a small spiritual Republic, created right in his room. Thus the little circle in the back-room of the bookshop in the Rue de la Fabrique and its diligent preliminary work for national liberty has an eminent historical significance for the whole of Canada.

Looking back today, it is crystal clear that Canada, in the sense of a big modern nation, was only made possible by returning full national rights to the French-speaking citizen of the country. The reconciliation thus effected between the two ethnic groups marked the threshold of modern Canada.

Crémazie was more than a suitable figurehead for these literary and political groups. His burning patriotic disposition, not as a Frenchman but as a French-Canadian; his personality, free from all base instincts and desires; his vivacious wit; and last but not least his integrity; these things automatically made him the quiet storm centre of the battle. And busied with such matters, his poetic inspiration caught fire only at a later date, in connection with an active nationalism.

It is quite true that he produced some early poems in his youth, but they were so bad that he was ridiculed when reciting them. One of his contemporary critics remarked that apparently Crémazie had been quite successful in making prose out of poetry. He was bursting with ideas, but their poetic expression certainly was not easily obtained. He needed years of experience and training before his instrument would sound clear and true—and then he would use it chiefly for patriotic songs, both gay and sad. His first poem well known to the reading public, 'The Battle in the Orient', dealt with events of the Crimean War. On first thoughts, the subjects would have had little interest for Canada; actually the reverse is true: it ended a long period of controversy between England and France, and in this war—for the first time—troops of both nations fought side by side on the battlefield.

Such a historically important change ought also to have

ended the controversies between English- and French-Canadians, or at least to have lessened them, and changed them into co-operation discussion and action. Crémazie expressed such a hope in the following part of the poem, addressed to both nations:

> 'Guarding the rights of nations, O exalted sentinels!
> You have fulfilled your noble mission
> Without fear of the threats of tyrants;
> You have received the palms of your glory,
> And all the people bless the resounding names
> Of exalted France and Albion.'

In the year 1855 a French man-of-war visited the port of Quebec for the first time since the British had been in power. The ship carried a mission sent to renew relations of friendship and trade between Canada and France. Crémazie, overjoyed, found expression for his feelings in his poem: 'The Old Canadian Soldier'. He had now become the kind of poet who uses his fine instrument not only for political occurrences, but also for events and impressions of more general human value. The Catholic memorial of All Souls inspired him in November, 1856, to a poem named 'The Dead' which deserves particular notice for its apparent conjecture as to his own future:

> 'Pray for him who, in exile far from his homeland,
> Perishes without hearing a single word of compassion;
> No one will offer up a prayer, or shed the gift
> Of a tear for his grave in a strange land.
> Who thinks of the unknown who sleep underground?'

Certainly, his mild poet's soul did not interpret his national feelings with a wild chauvinism. His dislike of excessive nationalism was expressed in the poem 'Peace', written in 1857:

> 'Today the serene goddess of Peace reveals the source of
> her bounty,

Both to vanquisher and vanquished alike, and offers to
them
The sweet stores of the homeland dear to their memory
Yesterday ruled the terrible majesty of war:
Today we celebrate the happiness of Peace.'

He expresses himself with the same clarity in his 'Song of the
Mohammedan', appearing in the same year:

'Now, seeing in the distance the beautiful horizon
As it lies before them, all the people renounce
For evermore from this day the slaughter of brother by
brother,
Forging ahead towards the future, with their heavenly
guides
Dressed in robes of divine light: Labour and Peace.'

It goes without saying that it would be wrong to compare the
poetry of Octave Crémazie with the work of Lamartine or a
Goethe. If such a comparison were made, the result would not
be favourable. But at the same time an unforgivable error
would have been committed: the significance of the poet
would have been considered in isolation from the impact of
his poetry on the fate of French Canada. This, above all, is the
value of his work. Crémazie and his poetry are not only the
true mirror of all the fears and hopes, the pride and suffering
of a people; for at the same time, the poet was, in his days, a
flaming example for his people on the road to freedom from
national oppression.

For this reason alone Crémazie attains the dignity of a
classic, and his works become an inseparable part of that what
is called world literature. Anyone carefully studying the
Canadian history of that period must find with a good
measure of surprise how much pride, joy and hope became
manifest in the critical year 1858 amongst the upper classes of
Quebec when the national epic song 'The Banner of Carillon'
was published. The poem evokes the spirit of glorious, bygone
days, then almost buried out of sight under the load of

national grief, when the banner of French settlers, enthusiastically traversing the whole North American continent, was seen alike in the valleys of the St. Lawrence and the Mississippi:

> '. . . The days of Carillon, when
> Under the white banner proclaiming our victories,
> Our forefathers earned a name of immortal renown,
> And traced with their own swords in the pages of history
> The record of their fame.'

Only when the reader penetrates to the historical significance of the poet will he understand his true meaning. When a nation is not decadent, the magical touch of a great poet is able to evoke from history: 'The world of glory, where our ancestors lived . . .'.

In this sense, Crémazie became the father of Canadian national poetry, to use the words of another Canadian poet, Abbé Casgrain. It was the logical choice to celebrate, in poetic form, the advent of June 15th, 1859, two hundred years after Monsignore Laval—perhaps after Champlain the most important personality of French-Canadian history—landed in Quebec. With his coming the real spiritual and Christian development of France's colony began. He was a priest of exceptional culture, remarkable activity and lofty morals; it was chiefly owing to his influence and perseverance that a large number of schools, churches and societies were founded, which nowadays form the basis of the country's civilisation. Therefore said Crémazie:

> 'He is not a well-known hero of world history,
> A man who comes to us in the splendor of victory,
> And who in Quebec puts down the sword of glory.
> He to whom on this day of joy our people carries
> Its thankfulness and tenderness,
> Is a gentle young man with friendly eyes.'

In practical life extremes often meet; this fatality has been encountered by all mortals. The excessive measure of his national enthusiasm and of his antipathy for the British rule perhaps led to Crémazie's deep admiration for Napoleon. In 1860 he wrote a poem, 'The War in Italy', speaking highly of the severe battles and victories of Magenta and Solferino. Crémazie was a devout Catholic; the victor of Magenta and Solferino, however, was not, and the irony of history has willed that it was precisely these victories which were attained in alliance with the freemasons of Piedmont, against the one major conservative catholic State, still existing at that time in Europe: Austria. It was therefore for the false side Crémazie wrote ecstatically: 'The day of Solferino! Only the great Homer could do thee justice; O murderous battle. . . .'

The true conception of these events is limited for us by the facts of history. Civilised nations of today fortunately do not seem to have much taste for the joy of deadly battles. Nowadays—an example is the attitude of the U.S.A.—humanistic thoughts make that nations—not always their leaders—have a clearer idea of the terrible sufferings and destructions that follow in the wake of such 'glory'. For a reasonable people, war is only warranted as a defence of freedom, of the own country, home and family against open or hidden foreign attacks. But for the rest, it would not be justified to make in his time our poet seriously responsible for this mentioned berserk poeticising. To come to this conclusion we only have to look again at this somewhat short-sighted fat man, with his jovial friendly face and who, most probably, never harmed a mouse. We look also on his lengthy poem, written in the same year, called 'The Thousand Isles', which is made in a friendly bucolic and patriotic vein. It seems to us extracted from the 'Thousand and One Night' tales and takes us to famous and beautiful spots on our earth, from the Alhambra to the shores of the Nile and the River Ganges, and which finally arrives at the conclusion that to the Canadian (in this special case, the French-Canadian of the Eastern Provinces) there is nothing more beautiful on earth than the St. Lawrence River:

> 'O shores, where the graves of our fathers
> Eternally speak to us of bygone years,

You alone utter the dear words which make
A Canadian heart thrill with yearning'.

Only it is that time did not stop at the shores of this
majestic stream, in itself a symbol of fleeting life; it stopped
neither for the poet nor before the little world around him. He
himself had become more mature, as is proved by the increasing clarity, purity and deeper meaning of his work, now showing a more profound philosophy of life. Crémazie, the man,
was richer in life's experiences and poorer in youthful ideals
and illusions. He had already learned what can be expected
from the integrity, faithfulness and friendship of human
beings, and made him cling even more to his national ideals.

The back-room of his bookshop was, as has already been
noted, the meeting place and centre for discussions of the
upper ten in the city, who were deeply concerned for their
compatriots political and cultural fate and who were ready to
sacrifice all for national freedom. This was the circle which,
with the eminent spiritual and material help of Crémazie, had
succeeded in initiating the 'French Canadian Institute' which
was to prove of the highest importance for the cultural progress of the French-speaking Canadian people. It was unavoidable that amongst the visitors there should be those who
did not particularly care for national ideals, and were out for
financial gain alone. To this group belonged a number of
quasi-politicians who certainly did not visit the poet for his
personal qualities but who were magnetically attracted by the
cash-box of the bookshop, always well filled with money.
There is no doubt today that these men know how to profit by
the inexperience and good nature of Octave Crémazie, who
represented the weakest point in the chain of the business
organisation. They succeeded in enmeshing him in an ever-
tightening net of endless financial commitments. Crémazie
was not without seeing the facts and he certainly perceived
the possible consequences, but this knowledge came too late to
save him.

It seems to be that his last, best, and poetically most valuable book, 'The Promenade of the Three Dead', was darkly premonitory of approaching doom. As his friends did not perceive visible indications of this, they failed to understand his work and felt that the poem was simply the product of the macabre timely determined disposition of the poet. This important and extensive poem was begun in 1861 and remained unfinished, but the available text of the first part of this 'Unfinished Symphony' of death proves that, by the passing away of Octave Crémazie, Canada has lost a poet not merely limited to the creation of patriotic verse, but a great artist of a deep psychologic poetry. His death occurred at the moment when he was on the point of giving to his people, his country and the literary world at large a series of impressive and matured works. No better proof can be offered than the fact that literary critics all showed the greatest concern for the first part of the poem when it was published in 1862, in the 'Soirées Canadiennes'.

Of course there are also negative critics. The first to aim his darts at the poem was Professor Thibault, who published his criticism in the 'Courrier du Canada'. This learned man was particularly incensed by the fact that Crémazie, in 'The Three Dead', had failed to follow the examples of classic poetry as well as the recipes of patriotic pamphlets, in order to create a romantic, modern work based only on general human principles. Perhaps it is best to let Crémazie himself reply to this criticism, out of the sadness of his exile. In his letter of January 29, 1867, he addressed his good friend, Abbé Casgrain, from Paris, in the following terms: 'For Mr. Thibault, as for many of my countrymen, "The Banner of Carillon" is, as he himself puts it, an impressive historical poem. I believe I have already told you: in my opinion this "Banner", which has caused so much comment, is a poor product from the literary point of view. The success of this short poem lies only in the idea itself, whereas, in my opinion, the form of it has very little value. It must be confessed that in matters of poetry there is not a very refined taste to be found in our country. If you rhyme "glory" with "victory" a few times, and repeat the procedure with similar high-sounding words, adding a few terms such as "our religion", "our fatherland", "our laws", "the blood of our ancestors", and if you serve this whole mixture well heated on the flame of patriotism, you are certain of success, and everyone will tell you so. In my opinion, however, if I had nothing to show for my poetical ability but this unfortunate "Banner of Carillon", then my little reputation would already long ago have been dead and buried in the eyes of serious literary experts.' We do not know, that we could add anything of special value to this answer to Mr. Thibault.

Sympathetic criticism, not with reference to the work itself but to the moment of Publication, was supplied by his friends. For the immediate success of 'The Three Dead' it certainly was of considerable importance that very shortly before its publication, the 'Comedy of Death' by Théophile Gautier had made its appearance, a work likewise concerned with the medieval theme of a 'Dance of the Dead', and which greatly appealed to artists of that period.

The attempt of Crémazie was compared with talented Canadian historical novelists, who used the form of the novel to produce epics of Canadian history, somewhat similar to the work of Fenimore Cooper. This latter, as everybody knows, had given an unforgettable portrayal of the transition of the North American continent from the Indian to the white race in his classic 'Leather Stocking Tales'. The volume entitled 'The Last of Mohicans' certainly overshadowed all efforts of Canadian and other competitors. It should be remembered, however, that outstanding poetry has rarely been a success on its first appearance; almost all of it must await rediscovery. In imitation of the ancient Greeks one might say that jealous gods do not allow success to come until the authors have been dead for some time without notice by contemporaries. In this sense, the fate of 'The Three Dead' is certainly no exception, and the renaissance of this poem is only now on the way.

Obviously the beauty of the torso of this poem must considerably suffer on its translations into foreign languages. The part bearing the subtitle 'Fantasy' takes us on a foggy night of the first of November to the old graveyard of Quebec. It is the night of All Souls' Day and All Saints' Day and the poet sees the souls rising from their graves. They appear with their skeletons and enveloped in the white shrouds of the dead which flutter in the cold breeze like shreds of mist.

> 'Silently they go; only here and there their bones lament
> When a bush tears away the violet remainder of their flesh.
> Where they pass, the flowers droop on their stalks,
> A dog flees howling in senseless fear,
> And passers-by are overcome with strange trembling.
> As they glide past in a white column
> Their shrouds, stirring in the autumn breeze reveal flesh-less limbs.
> But three of them slacken their pace!
> Their bodies are almost whole, their faces less ghastly pale,
> As if they were the latest harvest of Death.'

These three are the persons whose fates Crémazie portrays. The first is an old man who left a son behind full of the joy of life; the old man knows that his son loves him even beyond the grave. The second is a young man swept away by death from his wife who, in her grief, desired to follow him into his grave. The third is a young man bewailed by his mother left behind. These three were acquainted during life and have met again in Death.

> 'They now for a few moments walk in silence;
> The sea, moaning as ever its sorrowful song,
> Sends its low lament skywards.'

The three travellers have just quickened their pace when the youngest suddenly addresses the old man:

> 'My friend, he says, I see a worm on your cheek that is devouring you,
> And when the wind plays in your whitened hairs.

> It seems that by his trembling he is afraid of losing his
>   pasturage.
> Tear of that worm and cover up your wounds,
> Else it will fright the living.'

Sarcastically, the old man asks him whether he believes that the Dead can arrive from their graves like pure white lilies or doves. Just as the spring has its roses, so Death has its worms, and the worm is the crown of Death. Then follows the dreadful and still most impressive dialogue between one of the Dead and the worm. Crémazie had a staunch Catholic belief. With entire conviction he believed that angels and demons manifest their existence on earth. The 'Enlightened' nineteenth century smilingly denied those things. The twentieth century, with the experience of the terrible fates of single individuals and whole nations, makes this form of belief appear less ridiculous than before. Crémazie also must have inherited many mystic and superstitious beliefs from his Breton ancestors. He never could abandon his opinion that the corpses of the deceased were not completely dead, but suffer gradually with their decay until they have returned to dust. For this purpose, of course, it must be assumed that the dead experience something of their earthly existence whilst in their graves:

> 'One day—was it day or night? I do not know,
> For the dead do not count the hours; for us
> There is but one day, and it is perpetual night—
> The satiated worms were asleep on my shroud.
> My grave was silent, but above, on the earth,
> I could hear Death reaping softly.
> Like a lonely miser who counts his gold
> I was counting my bitter grief and all my sorrows
> When suddenly I heard a despairful cry.
> A voice replied, forceful, angry,
> Of which the echo alone was enough to chill one's soul,
> Ominous as a knell ringing out in the night.'

The cries originated from one of the Dead, who had been

buried the day before and who for the first time was attacked by a worm:

> 'Where am I? What is it that bites me thus?
> My anguished body twists and turns
> Like a tree in a hurricane.
> Who is sharing with me my narrow couch?
> It is coming near me again: I feel his mouth
> Harrowing my side!'

Now the horrible menacing answer is heard, cynical and cold, although solemn at the same time:

> 'I am the master here! My breath is icy
> Like the wind of a wintry day.
> I overwhelm the mighty.
> I am King. I am the Worm.'

The recently dead are horrified: already the worm was tearing their flesh. Could they so quickly become the spoils of this terrible being, although only yesterday they had left the surface of the earth, lamented by all their relatives? Once again the dead man protests against such a fate, in accordance with Crémazie's conception that life has not yet been fully extinguished in the body.

> 'Alas if only I could fly from this place of horror!
> Perhaps if I cried out, an invisible hand
> Would pluck me out of my grave.
> There are many yet who walk above me—
> Help me! Save me!
> Not even an echo find the cries of my suffering.'

During this dialogue, the dead man seems to feel a warm tear touch his forehead. He immediately realises that this must be his loving mother weeping at his grave. Here Crémazie honours motherly love in beautiful verse put into the mouth of the deceased. But the worm interferes with these thoughts and answers with cold cynicism:

'Those blisful dreams enjoyed on the earth above,
So alluring and so beautiful,
Shatter like glass in my domain,
At the impact of cold realty.
No, this drop of water is not a gift
That follows one who has just died;
Nor this heartbreak, which weaves a crown
With the painful leaves of memory.
It is only an ally sent by the earth
To hasten your destruction;
The earth, who shares the prey with me,
And who always takes the lion's share.'

When however, during this despicable address to the dead man the worm confessed that the elements of the transient state are also transient themselves, and that the worm itself must die, a sensation of wild elation and high contentment is experienced by the deceased:

'Like us thou shalt die! A! Death, our queen,
Shall also wipe thee out with her sovereign hand
As a press crushes fruit.
Who in this gloomy kingdom can ever tell us
Which is the thing most terrible to see:
The corpse of a worm, or of a man?'

Returning to gentler feeling, the deceased desires that his dust, through the circular course of the elements which he now accepts as unavoidable, will eventually be transformed into a flower to be gathered by the devoted hands of his mother and put, as an offering, on the altar of the Lord. With undiminished hate the worm tries to destroy even this illusion, so that the deceased, moved by terror, cries out:

'Fiends! Hell! Damnation! Am I dreaming in my grave?
Is it the cry of the vulture devouring
The tender dove just torn from her nest?
The eye of Satan glistens in the darkness
When this unspeakable tale is sung,

As black as the hell of an endless nightmare.'

In this fashion the old man ends his story amongst the three dead. Now it is the young man's turn and he confesses to the older man:

'This blighted corpse, this, refuse of nature,
This purulent filth serving as a nourishment for the worm,
This dead thing to which the worm cries "I am King here!"
This mountainous abomination of shame and misery,
This pathetic child who believed in his mother's tears:
O my companions of the grave, this corpse, it is I!'

With this confession, and with the doubt as to what to believe in the motherly love and all the beautiful sensations and feelings which had warmed his heart during his span of life on earth, or the cynicism of the worm—the first and only part of the poem ends.

In a letter of the year 1867 addressed to his friend Abbé Casgrain, Crémazie outlined his plan for a second and third part of the poem, which, however, he was never to complete. Now the three Dead, each one separately, visit their families. The father finds his son, who he though had loved him so dearly, in wild orgies and slandering his father's name. The husband finds his wife already flirting with his successor. Only the young man finds his mother, overwhelmed with grief, in her room praying for his soul. In this way the dramatic 'Dance of the Dead' finds a shining consummation in the beautiful Christian element of a mother's love, constant beyond the grave.

When writing this sceptical poetry—not all flattering to the fidelity of friends and the love of husbands—Crémazie must have been strongly depressed by the anger he felt with regard to the cowardly attitude of those who encouraged him to embark upon various financial ventures and then left him entirely alone. The catastrophe came in the autumn of 1862; debts had been mounting to meteoric proportions and, in accordance with the barbaric laws of the period, Crémazie was forced with the possibility of lifelong imprisonment. But his exploiters were moved by strong feelings of apprehension, as they feared that legal proceedings might unveil many things which they preferred to keep hidden. They forced him to flee on the night of the 12th of November, and to hide himself in Paris under the name of Jules Fontaine.

The solemnity of Crémazie's character becomes clearly apparent when one learns how very heavily his exile weighed upon him. Apart from a few poems written for special occasions, his poetic vein seems to have dried up under his misfortunes. In Paris he lived through the siege of the city as well as the famine, which formed the subject of a book worth reading even today. He found himself almost without income. Sometimes he succeeded in earning some money at odd jobs; some old friends helped him temporarily, amongst them the poet Abbé Casgrain in Quebec, who—through his undying friendship, not only for the rich book-merchant, but also for the poor exile—has earned himself the enviable reputation of never forgetting his friends.

Crémazie died in dire poverty on the 16th of January 1879, in a small hotel room in Havre, 'lonely in life, lonely in death', as he himself, long ago, had written prophetically. He was buried in the named city, but it has not been possible to find the place of his grave.

Charles Mair

Not Samuel Marchbanks but Samuel Johnson once sceptically stated: 'Patriotism is the last refuge of the scoundrel'. That was eighty years before the birth, in a town of five hundred souls including a settlement of retired Peninsular and 1812 war veterans, of Charles Mair, later not only to wave the flag of Empire with the lustiest of Upper Canada Loyalists, but also with the earliest of the settlers to carry it energetically into the region of what is now Winnipeg. The Algonquin Indians still thrived in the forests of the Upper Ottawa valley when Mair as a boy spent his spare time hunting and fishing there—followed in and out of season as he tells us—and at swimming, quoit play, racing, snow-shoeing, trapping, maple-sugaring, and the old Scotch shinty, a precursor of ice-hockey.

Growing up as he did with the country in a locality where the forward movement of civilisation was apparent in the giant removals of forest and increasing industrialisation of the larger towns, he decided to move West and chronicle his country rather than take a medical degree. Mair was, in fact, a survival of the pioneer period in an age of eastern consolidation and political entrenchment, and given the talent it was inevitable that he should want to record in verse and prose his own consciousness as well as the evidences about him of a growing national spirit. The enthusiasm he showed in any undertaking —he must have been aware of the old adage: 'God is a rewarder of adverbs, not of nouns'—proved infectious to those about him so that not only did he give to his verse an energy and vast stride of conception which is one of his essentially Canadian characteristics, but he also earned Canadian fame in his own lifetime.

Before the war of 1812 and the rebellions of 1837 forced a realisation of the need for unity on the Maritimes and the two Canadas, they were regions largely isolated economically, politically, and socially. Mair consciously dealt with a Canadian subject matter which was common to all these communities, and his drama 'Tecumseh' was based upon an event which above all others up to that time effectively awakened a spirit of single heartedness, single mindedness, and single endeavour—the defence of the northern colonies by General Brock. Mair was, therefore, a fighting nationalist both in poetry and in action, and a pattern of the forward-looking Confederation man; it follows that his poetry, in representing the sentiment of a united Canada—his first volume was published the year after Confederation—was amongst the first to reflect a Canadian individuality rather than a merely regional one. On the other hand, Mair had little knowledge of French-Canadian literature, and although he daily rubbed shoulders throughout the first half of his life with French-Canadians, yet he too completely typified the liberal English-Canadian Tory view to qualify completely as a national poet.

Mair, however, is the only other Canadian poet with Sangster who by 1870 had published poetry directly and deeply national rather than regional or cosmopolitan in matter and sensibility. Isabella Valancy Crawford, first among Canadian lyric poets with Carman and Lampman before the twentieth century, did not publish 'Old Spookses' Pass, Malcolm's Katie, and other Poems' at her own expense until 1884; Roberts' first volume 'Orion, and other Poems' appeared in 1880; while to look backwards, Charles Heavysege, a better poet than either Sangster or Mair, a Canadian poet although not arriving in Montreal from England until he was thirty-seven years of age, does not qualify as a nationalist since he dealt exclusively with universal moral impulses. And French-Canadian poetry, according to Jan Forbes Frazer, was at this time characterised by five main themes of thought and action: 'pride in the group; love for an idealised, classical, pre-revolutionary France; strong in the moral principles of the counter-reformation; veneration for the institutions of the Roman Church and the family; preservation of the language and folklore; and the cult of the soil, whose inevitable by-product was literary regionalism'.

Nationalism accompanied romanticism in this period, deriving ultimately from Rousseau and Châteaubriand, and was untouched until after the First Great War by the naturalism of Flaubert and of Jack London's short stories. In America, however, the latter movement was in full swing. In 1890 there were more strikes than in any other year of the century, and foreclosures on farmlands drove angry thousands westward. Increased productivity had not brought the golden age, and the seamy side of life forced itself on the attention of such writers as Stephen Crane, Lincoln Steffens, and Hamlin Garland, ending in the establishment of a 'muck-rake school'.

In Canada the tale was different, since writers were more concerned with national unity and national consciousness than city stews and unemployment. Embarrassing questions were being asked, indicative of the deep social unrest productive of naturalism in literature, but which should have been rooted more firmly in popular movements before infiltrating into the literature. Why these endless distinctions between Catholics and dissenters? Why are women forced to labour for half the pay of men? Why does not the Church try applied Christianity? Our higher classes are allowed to remain in control of public office; why not try the fresh blood of the lower classes, who are not in any alliance with foreign bankers? Why should education be denied the large people simply because it is in the self-interest of cliques to withold the privilege?

Such were the roots of the bitter controversy conducted towards the close of the century by Canadians of all classes, national and racial origins. An added cause of unrest was the callous overriding of the western settlers who called upon Riel to help them in 1885, while on his being hanged Catholics and Orangemen flew at each others' throats. McDonald's trans-Canada-railway scheme involved monstrous scandals; and until the year before the Yukon gold rush a world-wide depression raged. These were all matters working for realism if not naturalism in literature and fine arts, but the closest approximation was in the nature realism of the native tradition group. Mair's 'Tecumseh' skirts psychological and social realism although the opportunity was certainly there for it, and in the remainder of his work he displayed none of the modern sensibility either anthropological or psychological.

Zola was right when he had written 'Naturalism does not belong to me, it belongs to the century. It acts in society, in the sciences, in letters and in art, and in politics.' But neither Taine's determinism nor Freud's preoccupation with the under-mind awakened interest amongst Canadian writers or artists of the time. Why was this so especially in the light of the Americans' deep cosmopolitan and national uneasiness? The answers probably lie in the simple fact that Canada had not grown up as fast as America. The latter had been a political nation for over a century, and had had a cultural unity for slightly less than that period, by the time the Canadian Pacific railway was completed. In 1891 the Dominion census showed a population of under five million for the whole of Canada, while the United States had twice that number during the War of 1812. America had taken the turn from romanticism after the Civil War, up to which time there had indeed been a strong romantic period of writing culminating in Whitman's ninety-page 1855 'Leaves of Grass'. Canada had no civil war, and the rebellions in each of the two Canadas had come too early to act as a revelatory maturing force on the national body; it took the 1914–1918 war to shake the stranglehold of literary romanticism.

The first Canadian poet to reveal a romantic, in contrast to a neo-classic, approach to nature was Charles Sangster, whose 'The St. Lawrence and the Saguenay and Other Poems' in 1856 preceded Mair's 'Dreamland' by only twelve years. Mair's first volume is a medley of unconscious reminiscences and direct borrowing, principally from the early Keats—whose 'Sleep and Poetry' is excerpted for a motto—Tennyson and Bryant. At the time of publication he was thirty years of age, and in accordance with contemporary tastes his reading had been directed by his mother and John Macintyre, Principal of Perth Grammar School, to romantic and neo-romantic poets. As a boy he had read Spenser and proceeded to Chaucer, Mallory, Chapman and Shakespeare. In his father's library he found the Canadian 'Literary Garland', a journal wholly devoted to stories and reviews of a diluted romantic nature, while during his Queen's University years he had a further opportunity to read extensively in the poets appealing to him.

After a break from the Arts course, during which time he worked at his father's square timber business and even served long enough in the Perth branch of a bank—one week—to convince himself that 'open air life' suited him better, he returned to study medicine. It was his intention to qualify as a doctor and proceed to the Red River Settlement, where he would combine medical practice and fur trading. It was while at Queen's this second time that he wrote most of the poems for the 'Dreamland' volume.

Only a few copies were distributed, the remainder being lost in one of the fires so frequent in the early days of the heavy firing necessitated by Canadian winters; but the slim volume dedicated to the wife of the Hon. William McDougall who was to engage Mair later the same year to accompany a westward bound surveyors' party, received several enlogistic reviews in Canadian newspapers, one by the eldest son of Judge Haliburton of 'Sam Slick' fame. Haliburton's review was both liberal in its praise and typical of the sentimental literary cliché and vapid diffusiveness indulged in by Canadian reviewers of the period, and still only too prevalent today even in our cities. He saw Mair as 'a young poet, who, though not long out of his teens, has accomplished enough to make us hope for a good deal more from his pen. When he was first pointed out to us, he appeared as brimful of fun and frolic as a schoolboy, and we could not help thinking that he looked as if cricket or croquet, boating and flirting, were more likely to be engrossing his thoughts than the quiet mysteries of nature of which he is, judging by the volume before us, an ardent and thoughtful student. The sunshine that pervades his poems is refreshing. Many poets, when they look upon Nature, are too prone to view it by the pale moonlight; and the voice that comes to us from their muse, is far too solemn and sad to be an echo of that song of Nature which, to the ear of the healthy and happy, is as cheery and joyous as the carol of the songbird.'

The echoes in these early poems of Mair's reading were also noticed by the critics, and it is this factor which most seriously detracts not only from the present poems but also from the 'Tecumseh' and 'Canadian Poems' of a decade later. The Dreamland poems are strewn with false diction and cumbersome phrase which have little root in sensitive thought and feeling deriving from the object without intermediary filters of preconceived response. Typical of his time, Mair was more concerned with the aura or general mood of a poem than with its intellectual and nervous fibres and cells; a phrase need not be exact, much less a word, so long as it contributed to the tone desired.

Only too often Mair does not, cannot, see the object for the beam of prior self-appointed abstraction in his eye. The result is a kind of unintentional dishonesty which imposes an illusion upon the reader by means of language chosen to represent the wished-for sentiment rather than one which would have been aroused by direct intercourse with the poetic object. Most of the poems in his first volume are defective for this reason: they are exercises in sentimental indulgence—with the exceptions noted below. A typical sonnet, 'Love's Empery', will illustrate the point:

> 'O Love! If those clear faithful eyes of thine
> Were ever turned away there then should be
> No heav'nly looks to take the gloom from mine,
> Nor any hills, nor any dales for me,
> Nor any honeyed cups of eglantine,
> Nor morning spilth of dew on land or sea.
> No sun should rise, and leave his eastern tent

To wake the music of the rambling wave,
Nor any freshness of the West be sent
To sweep away the night's savours of the grave.
But when I gaze into those fadeless eyes,
Me thinks I am in some mysterious land,
Where far-off seas take colour from the skies,
And voiceless on a mountain-top I stand.'

Here is an artificial situation treated in vicarious terms. The subject is as given in the poem—the extent and power of love. But the poem is consciously imitative of Keats—the last four lines are a direct echo from 'One First Looking into Chapman's Homer'—and any thought of immediacy of experience is denied by the derivative coinage of tired poetic clichés. Neither is their any indication in the poem that Charles Mair Canadian of the third quarter of the nineteenth century, saw or felt directly and on his pulses, anything at all connected with his subject, in terms of the life about him, the language spoken, the sensitive habitual thought of men in that time and place. There is nothing to strike and pierce home to the reader: it is life as experienced via Keats and Tennyson at his worst.

But the reader may well ask: why this severity? Why so hard on a pioneer of Canadian literature, who after all spent his youth in the woods and on the streams, in a society barely removed from frontier conditions? Why bother to seriously discuss the first versifiers of a culture barely emerged from the forests and wooden settlements of its birth, and aspiring to letters at all only in so far as it is derivative? For these were the conditions, even though Confederation took place a year previous to the publication of the book. It is too often assumed that by 1867 Canada was already 'civilised'. Perhaps it is only necessary to swell the chorus of hitherto ineffective complaint by reminding ourselves that both Montreal and Toronto today, cities of more than a million inhabitants, have but one professional theatre each, one art gallery each, and that apart from the CBC, independent radio stations right across the Dominion spend a large part of each day praising the merits of washing soaps and easy-loan finance companies.

Mair was writing poetry, then, under primitive cultural conditions which forced him to look to England for his poetic fare and technique, and despite the fact that his first dominie liked Pope—but he never quoted poetry in class, or dealt with it—and that he read the classics at secondary school owing to intimacy with the principal. There was, of course, a strong pro-English bias in literary predilection, since Canada did not as yet have any consolidated social class of cultivated tastes, and since, therefore the tendency was to look nostalgically and reverently on the standards of the Victorian gentleman. And although many of that class in England owned a sensitive taste in a very broad sense, there was no rooted correspondence in Canada, and the yearning on the part of Canadians for such merit only too often took the form of pretension and sentimental humbug.

Mair, in so far as he was unable to free himself from such pretension, was bound to write third-rate verse, just as those today who associate poetry with roseate dreams and nostalgic self-commiseration are bound to identify the poetic state with their own despairful or elated states of spiritual flabbiness. Such a fault is, of course, not limited to Canadian readers. Thus we are bound to examine the early poets with some care for two main reasons: the first, to disabuse readers of certain deadly preconceptions of the use and function of poetry, and the second, to prepare the way for a respectful, clear-eyed study of Canadian poets of the past.

But in addition to noting the tendency of Mair's time to view poetry as second-hand experience, we must remember that he was only thirty at the time, and that indications of considerable promise are present. There is first of all a sense of sureness in the handling of theme and structure, and the thought, generously conceived and rounded, is expressed with ease and in a straight-forward manner. In 'Prologue to Tecumseh', a poem showing either that he had begun to think about the drama he was to publish eighteen years later, or that he had read John Richardson's poem of the same title, he

uses Indian names—a unique North American note—with
Miltonic ease:

> 'Amidst the throng
> Powhattan comes, Tomocomo the strong,
> Bold Wingina and lofty Ensenore.
> What Wampanoag strideth quick before
> With haughty port? This great Massassoit!
> The cunning Uncas hastes, his dark eye lit
> With fury, and from Pokanoket's glade
> Canonchet, too, the last, the lost has strayed
> With hapless Weetamore.'

The Keatsian 'August' and 'The Firefly' give indications of
Mair's vivid perception of Nature and ease of expression, particularly the detailing in the former poem of insects, birds and
other animals:

> '. . . therefore the bee
> Wades knee-deep in the purple thistle tops,
> And shares their sweetness with the hungry wasp.
> Therefore the butterfly comes sailing down,
> And, heedless, lighting on a hummer's back,
> Soon tonks aloft in sudden strange alarm,
> Whilst bee and wasp quick scurry out of sight,
> And leave their treasures to the plodding ant.
> The beetle in the Tree-top sits and sings
> His brassy tune with increase to the end,
> And one may peep and peer amongst the leaves,
> Yet see him not though still he sits aloft.
> And winds his reedy horn into the noon.
> Now many a sob is heard in thickets dim,
> Where little birds sit, pensive, on the spray,
> And musc may hap on the delights of Spring;
> And many a chitmunk whistles out its fear,
> And jerks and darts along the pannelled rails,
> Then stops, and watches with unwinking eyes
> Where you to stand, as motionless as death;

CHARLES MAIR

But should you wag a finger through the air,
Or move a-tiptoe o'er the crispy sod,
Twill snudge away beneath the balsam brush,
Quick lost and safe among the reddened spray.
Now one may sit within a little vale,
Close to the umbrage of some wood whose gums
Give heavy odours to the heavy air,
And watch the dusty crackers snap their wings,
Whilst gangs of blue-flies fetch a buzzing teaze
Of mad, uneasy whirlings overhead.'

The greatest merit of the poems is that their composition obviously sharpened his senses and skill for certain passages of 'Tecumseh', and above all of his prose. Apart from this, the Canadian note is undeniably sounded, not merely in many of the subjects—an easy enough matter—but in the communication of the vastness of Nature, of continental extension and fecundity and wealth. And accompanying this is an aspiration of sentiment which finds its most satisfying embodiment in the heroic conception of the Indian chief, Tecumseh.

*　　　*　　　*

The first session of parliament representing the Dominion of Canada opened on the memorable day, November 7th, 1867. Lord Monck, in his speech from the throne, naturally enough emphasised the potentialities of the new union and its future expansion in numbers and area, and it was during this sitting that a movement originated for annexing the North-West. The Honourable William McDougall urged the mismanagement and misrule of the Hudson's Bay Company, together with the far from fictional fear of the United States, whose appetite had recently been whetted by an Alaskan hors-d'œuvre.

McDougall, Minister of Public Works in the new government, engaged Mair 'to collect and collate the evidence in the Parliamentary library, with reference particularly to treaties, and the question of the Company's title' then in dispute. It

72

was a matter of outlining the Hudson's Bay Company's claims to Rupert's Land and the North-West Territory, so that McDougall and Sir George Cartier could knowledgeably arbitrate with Company representatives in England. Mair confessed himself to be much interested in North-West doings and its literature, and his précis proved satisfactory. As a result, McDougall asked him along on the trip to England as secretary, but owing to a sister's severe illness Mair was unable to go.

But McDougall urged Mair to accompany a survey party to the Red River where they intended to plan an immigration road to the Lake of the Woods. Mair's task, in addition to acting as paymaster, was to describe the country—'a sealed book as yet to the Canadian people' as McDougall described it—in order to encourage westward expansion and general immigration. Letters on the trip appeared regularly in both the Montreal 'Gazette' and the 'Toronto Globe', letters successful in attracting interest to the West, and written in a racy, direct, fresh style, without pretension or obvious literary indebtedness. In fact, after a review of Mair's total prose output, one can without hesitation name him as one of the first important Canadian prose stylists and descriptive writers, as the following excerpt from 'Through the Mackenzie Basin' may testify: 'In the 6th, a lovely fall morning, we bade goodbye to Wahpooskow, its primitive people, and its simple but ample pleasures. Autumn was upon us. Foliage, excepting in the deep woods, was changing fast, the hues largely copper and russet; hard body-tints, yet beautiful. There were no maples here, as in the East, to add a glorious crimson to the scene; this was given by shrubs, not by trees. The tints were certainly, in the larger growths, less delicate here than there; the poplar's chrome was darker, the willow's mettled chrome more sere. But there was the exquisite pale canary of the birch, the bloodred and yellow of the wild rose, which glows in both hues, the rich crimson of the red willow, with its foil of ivory berries, and the ruddy copper of the high-bush cranberry. These, with many other of the berry bearers and the wild-flowers, yielded their rich hues; so that the great pigments of autumn, crimson, brown and yellow, were everywhere to be seen, beneath a deep blue sky strewn with snowy clouds.'

The ultimate result of the McDougall-Cartier negotiations is well known—the transfer of the North-West Territory to Canada in 1870, and the payment of 300,000 livres sterling to the Company in exchange for its proprietorship. Mair had by this time reached the Red River Settlement, and fallen in love with Elisabeth Mackenney, Ontario niece to the doctor Schultz whose career had first decided him to take up the study of medicine. After a remarkable series of adventures, escapes, treks—one of which was to fall prisoner to Louis Riel and his métis rebels, escape under threat of being shot (one of Mair's companions was shot, thereby precipitating a furore of protest in the East) by crawling through a jail window, and make his way in disguise by horse and sled sixty miles to Portage la Prairie—Mair returned to Upper Canada. There he addressed large audiences on the subject of Riel's rebellion, the meetings having been arranged by the 'Canada First' organisation, by that time also known as the 'Twelve Apostles'. Especially successful was the Toronto meeting at which Mair and Doctor Schultz spoke, and it was largely due to their energy that the government finally dispatched Colonel Wolseley, later to become commander-in-chief of the British Army, to come to an end with the rebellion. Mair believed that this expedition was 'the second essential step towards the preservation of the West to Canada, and to the opening up of its illimitable possibilities to her people'.

The 'Canada First' movement had originated with a Toronto barrister, William Foster, and was designed to defend Confederation against declared and undeclared enemies. Mair was one of the first group of five members and it was perhaps largely owing to their persuasion that he discontinued his medical studies at Queen's University in order to accompany the survey party previously mentioned. He later wrote a poem in memory of Foster, eulogising the broad nationalism which strove to encourage the growth of a Canadian national sentiment at a time when—as he said—'provincialism of the narrowest type was rampant, and the very name "Canadian" was a jibe on both coasts'. Of little interest as poetry, significant in every word if considered in the light of the times, are the following lines:

'Throw sickly thoughts aside—
Let's build on native fields our fame;
Nor seek to blend our patriot pride
With alien worth or alien shame!
Nor trust the falterers who despond
The doubting spirits which divine
No stable future save beyond
Their long imaginary line!
But mark, by fate's strong finger traced,
Our country's rise; see time unfold,
In our own land, a nation based
On manly deeds, not lust for gold.'

The stamping emphasis and simple iteration of principle of the words put into Foster's mouth gain high significance when seen against a contemporary offer in 1866 of ten million dollars for all Hudson's Bay territories in North America; while Senator Sumner could remind his Canadian auditors some time later—and as recently as ninety years ago—that the Alabama Claims discussion would hardly go on well as long as British settlers throughout 'this hemisphere, including provinces and islands', remained to precipitate Fenian antagonism.

And for the other side of the coin was the feeling, strong even in the 'Canada First' movement itself, that national character was only possible via national autonomy within a British Federation, autonomy at a time when America was bidding for half of Canada, and Canadian politicians were sceptically asking themselves who or what under heaven could save the union after Sir John A. Macdonald's death. It is just possible that Mair's reiteration of Imperialism in his poems and through 'Tecumseh', as well as in his prose, was at least partially intended to offset suspicions aroused by critics of the autonomy-conscious 'Canada First' movement. Similarly his later outcries against the Hudson's Bay Company, although doubtless indicative for the most part of altruistic nationalism, may have been influenced by his independent fur-trading. It is of interest in this respect to note the Canadian tory opinion of Jefferson as reflected in 'Tecumseh'; these keen Imperialists associated him with anarchic mob liberty:

> 'That foe, whose poison plant, false liberty
> Runs o'er his body politic and kills
> Whilst seeming to adorn it . . .
> . . . confounding Nature's order, setting fools
> To prank themselves, and sit in wisdom's seat
> By right divine. . . .'

After a wearisome expedition up Lake Superior and over five hundred miles of wilderness, following the route once marked out by fur traders, Wolseley's force arrived only to find Riel's band already dispersed. But even during its journey Manitoba had been officially accepted as a province into the Confederation, and many of the men remained on as settlers, to be followed by thousands of immigrants attracted by liberal land grants. Charles Mair was not only of the stuff of the makers of Canada, but in the case of Manitoba can be looked upon as himself a maker.

Following the escape of his wife, who had managed to slip by the Fenians and rebels disguised as a man in capote, cap and sash, the Mair's settled in Portage la Prairie for five years, principally engaged in fur-trading. After a later move to Prince Albert on the North Saskatchewan River, still near the frontier where he could feel:

> '. . . the strong friendship of primeval things—
> The rugged kindness of a giant heart
> And love that lasts . . .'.

Fear of the second Riel rebellion forced Mair to move his family to Windsor, Ontario. It was here that he wrote 'Tecumseh', which claimed the favourable attention of all Canadian critics. First published in 1886 it was republished in 1901 with a number of 'Canadian Poems' and dedicated 'to the survivors of the Canada First Association'. During these years he was employed in the Dominion Immigration Service, and finally appointed head of the department first at Lethbridge, Alberta, and later at Fort Steele, British Columbia. He also found time to write numerous reminiscences, and an excellent paper pleading for the preservation of the nearly extinct American Bison. This was read before the Royal Society and stimulated the Canadian Government to purchase a herd and establish it in Wainwright Park near Banff.

His knowledge of the bison and its way of life was extensive and acute, his remarks ranging from Indian curing of the hides and a survey of the disastrous effects of plain-hunting, to the derivation of the Indian buffalo dance, and a historical sketch of the species. His careful science and his vigorous and clear style are attested by the following report: 'When not grazing the favourite occupation of the animals was wallowing, a curious summer custom (for the bison did not wallow in winter) and which, from its frequency, seemed to have something of the nature of a sport, as well as a sanitary purpose. There are many great prairies on the Saskatchewan where these wallows literally touch each other in all directions. Thousands of animals engaged in the exercise at the same time, and seen at a distance, the dust raised by their writhing looked like pillars of smoke arising from innumerable fires. These wallows are sometimes confounded by newcomers with the "têtes des femmes", as they are called, or rough depressions and hummocks caused by fire penetrating and interlacing in the sod.'

Mair's papers on the bison and 'Through the Mackenzie Basin' should be required reading in every Canadian school. In 1899 Mair was appointed to accompany an expedition into the Peace River district to treat of a transfer of Indian territorial rights. Mair's long account of the trip is a brilliant piece of descriptive writing, of which the following report of a gala occasion bears out the statement that Mair is one of the finest prose stylists amongst earlier Canadian writers: 'But the two

dancing floors were the chief attraction. These also had been
walled and roofed with leafy saplings, their fronts open to the
air, and, thronged as they generally were, well repaid a visit.
Here the comely brunettes, in moccasins or slippers, their
luxuriant hair falling in a braided queue behind their backs,
served not only as tireless partners, but as foils to the young
men, who were one and all consummate masters of step-
dancing, an art which, I am glad to say, was still in vogue in
these remote parts. French-fours and the immortal Red River
Jig were repeated again and again, and, though a tall and
handsome young half-breed, who had learned in Edmonton,
probably the airs and graces of the polite world, introduced
cotillons and gave the calls with vigorous precision, yet his
efforts were not thoroughly successful. Snarls arose, and knots
and confusion, which he did his best to undo. But it was evident that the hearts of the dancers were not in it. No sooner
was the fiddler heard lowering his strings for the time-honoured
Jig than eyes brightened, and feet began to beat the floor,
including, of course, those of the fiddler himself, who put his
whole soul into that weird and wonderful melody, whose
fantastic glee is so strangely blended with an indescribable
master-note of sadness. The dance itself is nothing; it might as
well be called a Rigadoon or a Sailor's Hornpipe, so far as the
steps go. The tune is everything; it is amongst the immortals.
Who composed it? Did it come from Normandy, the ancestral
home of so many French-Canadians and of French-Canadian
song? Or did some lonely but inspired voyageurs, on the banks
of the Red River sighing for Detroit or Trois Rivières—for the
joys and sorrows of home—give birth to its mingled chords in
the far, wild past?'

During his last years at Victoria, British Columbia, Mair
contributed various articles and memoirs to newspapers and
saw himself commended throughout Canada as one of her
first authors. Queen's University conferred on him the degree
of LL.D. three years before his death in 1927, he having then
outlived his wife by twenty-one years, and having been preceded by three of his seven children.

It remains to look at 'Tecumseh', Mair's most significant poetic work, although of less literary importance than his prose. Pauline Johnson praised it highly along with his other reviewers, and Charles G. D. Roberts in his 1898 History described it as 'a thoroughly Canadian creation, full of sturdy patriotism'. It is that, and commendable for literary reasons as well, if not to the extent of contemporary critical encomium. The defects of derivative verse have already been discussed, and there is no need to consider them again in relation to a work of large conception and containing passages of poetic merit. Of 'Tecumseh', Mair claimed that: 'Its colouring, at any rate, is due to a lifetime's observation of those primitive inter-racial and formative influences which, together with a time-honoured policy, are the sources of the Canadian tradition', and confessed with shrewd insight that the war of 1812 was 'the turning point of Canada's destiny'. Against an invading army of five hundred thousand troops, Canada mustered a force of a few thousand to engage them successfully at Detroit and Queenston Heights, both Brock and Tecumseh, by their deaths in victory, uniting the wavering Canadians as they had not been before.

The plot is centred on Tecumseh's support of General Brock and his troops during the 1812 war. An extraneous love interest is supplied in the frustrated passion of Tecumseh's niece and the captive 'pale-face' Lefroy—extraneous because not intrinsically part of the main action, the tragedy of the Indian people as symbolised by Tecumseh. Tecumseh treats with General Harrison for all the Indian peoples, but the differences are irreconcilable. One of the finest passages is spoken by Tecumseh as a lament for the lost lands:

> 'Once all this mighty continent was ours,
> And the Great Spirit made it for our use.
> He knew no boundaries, so had we peace
> In the vast shelter of His handiwork.
> And, happy here, we cared not whence we came,
> ... Thus flowed our lives until your people came,

Since then our tale is crowded with your crimes,
With broken faith, with plunder of reserves—
The sacred remnants of our wide domain—
With tamp rings and delirious feasts of fire,
The fruit of your thrice-cursed stills of death,
Which make our good men bad, our bad men worse.
. . . Those plains are ours!
Those forests are our birth-right and our home!
Let not the Long-Knife build one cabin there—
Or fire from it will spread to every roof,
To compass you, and light your souls to death!'

Mair closely follows history in the Tippecanoe defeat of the Indians, and Tecumseh went North to join Upper Canada against the American armies. Brock's troubles are noted with care—the disloyal settlers recently from America; the procrastination of other Canadian leaders; the numerical insufficiency of his forces and supplies; the 'jarring needs of harvest-time and war' as they both draw on the man power; the low morale at one time during the preparations, due to 'England's vast war, our weakness, and the eagle whetting his beak at Sandwich with one claw already in our side'. The dramatist's detailed historical knowledge of the event is of the same order as his observations of the bison of Indian folkloric culture, of the country of the North-West. He had a remarkably keen eye, and an appetite for life which exulted in the minutest of details. Whether it is a description of a camping site or an Indian face, the ease of parturition of Indian women or the derivation of Indian names, the vivid picture comes through in both prose and the later poetry. We have already had excerpts from his prose; in the following, the poet-woodsman lover, Lefroy, describes his western trip with Tecumseh in terms which must have been a direct transcript of Mair's own journeys and which provide a foretaste of the vast sweep and pristine vigour of the poetry of E. J. Pratt. So Lefroy is writing:

'. . . . . We left

The silent forest, and, day after day,
Great prairies swept beyond our aching sight
Into the measureless West; uncharted realms.
Voiceless and calm, save when tempestuous wind
Rolled the rank herbage into billows vast,
And rushing tides which never found a shore.
... And sunless gorges, rummaged by the wolf,
Which through long reaches of the prairie wound,
Then melted slowly into upland vales,
Lingering, far-stretched amongst the spreading hills.'

Mair's sympathetic portrayal of the vicissitudes of the Indians by their conquerors' ruthless advances is at once moving and convincing and one of the best presentations in the play. The love story completes itself in the sacrificial death of Jena, although not justified in terms of dramatic interest because of Mair's seeming inability to vivify what only seem to be stock and wooden situations; it is relieved, however, by several passages of descriptive power. Striking lines are frequent, lines whose sentiment and imagery arises directly from the dramatic situation:

' .... Master of Life,
Endue my warriors with double strength!
May the wedged helve be faithful to the axe,
The arrow fail not, and the flint be firm!
That our great vengeance, like the whirlwind fell,
May cleave through thickets of our enemies
A broad path to our ravaged lands again.'

In the 1901 edition of 'Tecumseh' appeared a collection of 'Canadian Poems' written by Mair within the previous decade, and proving to be his last ventures in verse. They deal with Canadian themes and include a nature poetry evocative of the peculiar genius of the Canadian scene in accord with the then contemporary Roberts, Lampman, Carnian group of poets. The gravest faults of the school were derivative imagery and style and wearying celebrations of maple and sumach, snows and waterfalls; its merits included a clean, clear, and vigorous expression suited to the theme of embounded national energy and optimism in a vast country of unsurpassed natural beauty distinctly its own. Mair proved himself deeply moved time and time again by the magic of the Canadian scene, as the following passage from the 'Legend of Chileeli' shows:

> 'Again the flowers looked, as of old,
> Companionable, and the woods less cold.
> Again those wards of Nature, summer-bright,
> Seemed sentient creatures lapt in self-delight.
> And o'er the lake some fairy hand had drawn
> An amethystine glory, like the dawn
> Of some far morn in heaven; a haze which blent
> The solemn waters with the firmament
> In charmed suffusion, rifted by the day
> With dreamy lights, which faded far away
> In infinite perspective.'

It is a new beginning of the world, and the poet catches the beholder's fresh surprise and innocent uplifting of heart—sursum corda. In the preface to the 1901 edition of 'Tecumseh', Mair gave a succinct account of his own aims as well as those of the whole 'native tradition' school: 'Our romantic Canadian story is a mine of character and incident for the poet and novelist, framed, too, in matchless environment; and the Canadian author who seeks inspiration there is helping to create for a young nation that decisive test of its intellectual faculties and original and distinctive literature—a literature liberal in its range, but, in its highest forms, springing in a large measure from the soil, and "tasting of the wood"'.

Maria Chapdelaine

The military value of the Port of Brest was already known to the old Romans, who built a fortress at Penfeld bordering a bay framed by a steep coast. Strategically, this little fjord offered excellent protection for any navy. During the reign of Louis XIV new fortifications were constructed and it was here that France's most important military port gradually developed. It is only during recent times, when airpower and rockets have developed to such a remarkable extent, that the value of this stronghold near the sea has been contested.

During the last quarter of the nineteenth century Brest was, without any question, a symbol of the seapower and colonial might of the French Republic. From the big workshops on the sight shore of Penfeld proceeded the continuous music of the tools of a technological age, the pounding and whirring machines. The products of these shops and yards proudly floated offshore on the sea-roads: the grey steel colossus of the fleet. Moreover, merchant marine vessels in bright, friendly colours came and went, painting plumes of rusty smoke against the pale blue sky of Bretagne, discharging cargo and landing passengers from many foreign countries and filling the port with movement and life.

On the left shore of Penfeld, like the petrification of a bygone age, the old town was laid out in the shape of an amphitheatre with many crooked and narrow alleyways. The blocks of dwellings, cut by streets, seemed to form part and parcel of the steep cliffs of the coast. Surroundings of this nature will not remain without influence on the thoughts and actions of the people growing up in such a town. The twentieth century had as yet not begun and a large part of mankind was still ignorant of a way of life which would make them servants of the machines created by themselves. Nevertheless, wide breaches had been made in the more spontaneous natural romanticism of former times; new tendencies were on the march over the whole front.

Fundamental changes were noticeable in the ideals of the young people; the taste for romantic literature and for idealistic dreams receded into the background; the desire for action, a predecessor of the worship of labour, became evident. The need for play on the part of the young people of the towns finds its satisfaction in sports, and the longing for adventures is mixed with technical conceptions and considerations.

There is little interest now in the Round Table of the King Arthur, the aimless adventures of the intrepid Roland, the magic attraction of a Sleeping Beauty saved by a handsome prince; young hearts are now captured by a voyage of 'Twenty Thousand Leagues Under the Sea', or to 'Secret Islands', in a submarine outfitted with all the tools of modern technology. In addition, mankind has already embarked on a 'Voyage to the Moon' at least yet theoretically. Country life loses its poetic magic, and in its stead comes the magnetism of ever-growing cities. The differences between land and city widen, and Socialism rediscovers peasants as labourers. Youth likes to think in terms of quantities and horsepower. Contemplation of nature loses the poetic touch; it is only the grandiose dissipation in nature which remains as a source of surprise. Nature is not as yet scored by man for being useless, and still enjoys an independent existence, although opinions sometimes appear to the effect that things 'could have been done much better'.

After discovering the mechanics of the sky and calculating the course of the stars as a counterpart to the penetration of the atom, obviously the personal God reigning beyond the stars must become 'meaningless' and face gradual liquidation. The 'end-of-the-century' atmosphere steadily increases. The sunshine of the old conception of God has disappeared, but the world still glows in the twilight of its fire.

A shallow optimism is the comfort of those who lack any conception of what the future might bring. Nothing is known as yet with regard to the nature of the new 'gods', although these speak through the hoarse, vindicative voice of Karl Marx, the naturalistic pessimism of Emile Zola and the resignation of Anatole France. Gradually nations are transmuted into factories; material pleasures and the consciousness of the power of the individual are on the increase. There is some late romanticism, but it is not strong enough to open the doors of the backroom to which the soul has been banned by the intellect. An increasing political, economic and personal Imperialism heralds the crude, impatient period of the approaching twentieth century.

Such was the picture and the spiritual climate of the western world when Louis Hemon was born in Brest on the 12th of October, 1880. His cradle had a place from which, through the windows of his family home, one had a perspective of the grey, moving water of the harbour and the rocky coastline damp from the fog, the ships which arrived and departed, and the endles movement of a big seaport. The home itself was furnished with a certain homely elegance and good taste, which was only normal for a cultured and well-situated family. The father, Felix Hemon, was a professor and later received an appointment as General Inspector of Schools.

There is not much known with regard to the early years of Louis Hemon. We do know, however, that he learned easily and successfully, but that he inherited a certain measure of distrustful reserve from his Breton ancestors, which prevented him from being liked by his classmates. The same ancestors gave him a tendency towards day-dreaming, and it is said that he could remain for hours at a stretch on the rocks of the coast without moving, looking out over the waves.

Louis was slender and fairly tall, and even as a young lad he already had remarkable muscular strength. It is easy to see that he was attracted by all kinds of gymnastics, and particularly liked cycling, at that time quite a novelty. He obviously preferred his sports to his books, except those which contained stories of adventures in far-away countries. This does not imply that he neglected his mental development, as equally it cannot be said that all devoted young 'bookworms' later become scientists or authors. Hemon's early desire for adventure is, in itself, nothing out of the ordinary in view of his physical propensities and of the wide world-view of a seaport. His sister reports that he had a strong desire to be independent and that this caused him to feel a certain loneliness even as a child. In accordance with his father's wishes, Louis commenced his studies in the faculty of law at Paris University. He passed his exams with success, studied oriental languages, and finally entered the School of Colonial Studies. Meanwhile, the first shadows darkened the life of a family which so far had been undisturbed by tragedy: his older brother, who had served in the Navy as a midshipman, died after a short illness.

Louis had already entered on a literary career during his studies. In conformity with his preferences, he published a composition in 'Velo', a sports journal and obtained first prize. Apparently he felt himself under some kind of obligation after obtaining the prize, and continued to contribute to the same journal, later called 'Auto', right up to the end of his life.

The literary efforts of most young people of his age and background consist mostly of lyrical verse. But it was not in line with his nature, which was matter of fact and throughout his life prevented him having sudden passions. It seems logical to assume that such a cool perspective of life as his, such a realism, would eventually have placed him in a respectable position or even high office. But there must have been something in his makeup in opposition to such a picture, because the young man, to the distress of his family, developed the most unusual tendencies—unusual, that is, for the scion of middle-class people. When he was offered a career as a colonial employee he flatly declined. The bourgeois ideals of having a family and a place of his own, together with a security of existence, did not at all appeal to him. Possibly he was unable to accept anything so easily obtainable, and was opposed to anything which came to him of its own accord. Also, perhaps, now that he was free from the duties of his studies and the spell of his ancestral home, his bohemian nature came into its own.

The big highways of the world tempted him irresistibly; they were an intoxicant which made him forget everything else: home, family, a secure future, and all the happy possibilities of a secure middle-class existence. We are reminded here of Cornelius Krieghoff, who was likewise carried by the secret magic of wanderlust over the highroads of many countries, and finally over the sea to the same country portrayed by his brush that Hemon would later describe with his pen. Truly, such romantic natures form an exceptional race. Even when they manifest themselves as artists they do not seem to be fully aware of their artistic ability. They do not seem to feel called or chosen for an artistic career in the same way as do other painters, sculptors, poets and composers. Their art products seem to arise out of their own material needs. They differ from the conscious artist in that they hold no specific opinion of their work as art. It has a definite purpose: the picture or the manuscript is sold and it produces money. It is left for their own generation—and more often for the next—to become aware of the perfection and brilliancy of the jewel that the author carelessly dropped in the quicksand of his days.

If the phrase did not ring false, one would be tempted to say: here are the Proletarians of art. Like many professional artists they have to cope with everyday worries, but they rarely know the bitterness of self-complaint due to being misunderstood. At most they feel vexation with regard to the stinginess of their purchasers. Neither their hands nor their lachrymal glands have been refined and, superficially, their customs and habits are not different from those of the working class which earns its bread with the work of its hands. Whatever they may have learned and whatever may be their background, they still feel more at home in the atmosphere of sweating labour and exertion than in the surroundings of the 'white collar brigade'. The former seems to them more congenial and less complicated. It is therefore possible for them to harvest success which an unreal bohemian, an aristocrat like Charles Gill, cannot obtain.

Instead of accepting an office position which would have given him security at a regular income, Louis Hemon went to Britain under the pretext of learning the English language thoroughly. Actually, he already spoke it fluently before leaving, but his voyage was justified by the fact that later, when he left the country, he could speak English without a trace of French accent. No dependable information regarding his activities in England is available. It has been reported that he did little work at a desk, but stood at a factory work-bench producing wooden articles. Another version has it that he was active in agriculture. At the same time, however, he produced articles and novels for French, and possibly also for English, publications. Most of these appear under a pseudonym and cannot be identified as his products.

The only fixed point for judging his qualities as an author during this period is his novel 'Lizzie Blakestone', which has its action placed in English circles. The manuscript of the story was sent, as was his habit, to the editorial rooms of the 'Temps' of Paris, without his even taking the trouble to obtain a recommendation or introduction. This in itself is quite a feat when one remembers that this leading newspaper received literary productions from very prominent authors all over the world. The novel was read and accepted. In the opinion of the chief reader for the 'Temps', the work was written in simple language and was a minor masterpiece of observation.

By the end of 1911 Louis Hemon had grown tired of Europe. For the near future he had various plans. First of all he was inclined to go to Indo-China, a country which he knew at least theoretically through his studies at the university, and whose language was also known by him. In addition, the secrets of the Islam world had a strong appeal for him. But the decision was finally taken in favour of Canada, after he had heard many things about this big country from a young Canadian who made him familiar with details of its rivers and woods. Late in the fall of 1911 Hemon arrived in Quebec. He took up lodgings in the old part of town with a family that had been recommended to him by his informant. It would be wrong to assume that the young man, who so far was entirely unknown, arrived in Canada as a distinguished traveller or as a more or less official French author. Hemon landed in Quebec as a completely unknown immigrant, and his first excursions were aimed not at any well-known personalities in public life, but simply in order to obtain work.

The period chosen for this project was most unfavourable. In one way and another the shadow of the terrible storm which was to ravage Europe in 1914 had already in anticipation blackened economy and life in the world. For the purpose of obtaining work Hemon made a short trip to Montreal, but returned to Quebec dissatisfied. Here he obtained information regarding the life of the settlers at St. John's Lake, a frontier where civilisation slowly progressed northwards against the wilderness. It was said that able hands could always find work in that area. He was looking for both bread and adventure, and so he went to Peribonka where he obtained work with a lumber company till the early summer of 1912. During his sojourn there he produced a realistic novel called 'Maria Chapdelaine', which has not only great poetic value but gives also a faithful portrayal of the life of the Canadian settler at this frontier.

None of the discordant social sounds of most of the novels of this period are heard in this work. The action opens in the small wooden church of the village of Peribonka, filled to capacity with faithful parishioners whilst the priest solemnly intones his 'Ite missa est'. The congregation leave the church while the final tones of the little organ fade away, and gather in the snow-covered church square bordered by wooden cabins. This is the right moment for a friendly chat and for listening to the town crier who, substituting for a daily newspaper, proclaims the news.

Gradually the crowd, all wearing their Sunday fur coats, disperses, and such settlers as came from far away to attend Mass put their horses to their sleds for the home journey. It will not take long before they disappear into the hills which frame the village, and into the snow-covered woods through which glistening tracks will lead them to their homesteads. After the religious service the church square, so quiet during weekdays, had become unusually animated by so many figures characteristic of the area and completely in harmony with the surroundings. After reading a few pages, we find that we are exceptionally well acquainted with these people in the snowy village, so far away from the big cities and so near to the impenetrable woods.

We make the acquaintance of the heroine of the story, Maria Chapdelaine, with her father and mother, and of the intrepid, restless woodsman François Paradis. The sleigh of the Chapdelaine's glides along the homeward road; the village is already far behind and soon the last homes of the settlers disappear. The road becomes rougher until finally it is hardly more than a track through the woods. The home of the family is at the end of the road, the utmost frontier in the woods. During the trip the author introduces us to a scene of exceptional dramatic quality. The Peribonka, in summer a foaming mountain river hurrying down amongst the rocks, is fully frozen during the severe winters of northern Quebec. But winter is almost past; it it shortly before Easter and the warm winds have already caused the ice to crack. In order to get home the party has to cross the river. For a moment the father rests his horse and scrutinises the white expanse of ice before him. He notices that the snow is already fairly soft, and realises that the thaw of spring weather is on its way. Then he urges his horse on. The icy surface cracks ominously under the weight of the sleigh; here and there the runners cut a dangerous groove into the ice; the surface moves and becomes noisy, and the nervous horse starts galloping. Foaming, sweating, and at the end of its strength it finally pulls the sleigh onto firm ground at the opposite shore, while behind them, in the middle of their track, they notice a black spot which increases in size: the open water! Father Chapdelaine looks back and critically contemplates the river. Without any sign of emotion he remarks thoughtfully to his family: 'I think we have been the last to cross the ice this winter . . .'.

Hemon now allows us to witness the life of the Chapdelaine family in their primitive log cabin, framed by woods and a few small fields. It is a hard and lonely life. Here it is that we fully appreciate the touch of master; the author knows how to sketch his persons and their fathers so lightly that the reader's train of thoughts leave soon for all kinds of inferences, although he cannot help but participate fully in the lives of the characters. Without being pressed, we become deeply aware of the mental contrasts which arise in such a community, far away from the rest of the world, contrasts which at the same time represent problems native to the area.

Mother Chapdelaine would have preferred to remain down below, near the village where they had formerly lived and where her husband had cleared trees to make room for the sowing of grain. It was so pleasant to have neighbours; every now and then came to visit her, and nearby the new little church had been erected. This good woman speaks the language of the longing and waiting of many thousands of conservative farmers, who had left the mild climate of western France behind and settled in this hard, strange country. Her husband and François Paradis, however, certainly do not belong to this category. They have restless souls; their enemy is the forest and they destroy it as they can. As soon as they achieve their purpose to some small extent, as soon as a small part of the forest has given way to farmland attracting new settlers who start to build their own homes and eventually a church, the former feel irritated by the accompanying establishment of peace and quiet which are a part of a community settlement. They then sell their holdings and proceed northwards, nearer to the virgin forest, in order to start their hard battle all over again, mesmerised by dangers and hardships.

'It is a good life for those who love farmlands', father Chapdelaine used to say, 'but it would not give me happiness.'

With such words, and with a touch of regret for the impossibility of leading a more settled life himself, he used to reject the chance of a quiet and less adventurous existence. Pioneers working at the frontiers of the forest form a race quite apart from organised human society and are urged on through life by secret forces which permit no rest. Amongst them will be found a wonderful type of man, to whom the normal values of good and bad do not mean much in his gigantic battles with Nature. Apart from the question as to how far such men are good or bad, it might seem reasonable to ask to what extent they are useful. Is it really necessary to destroy the forest as they do? Did not the Indians lead a relatively happy life under its massive green roof?

More farmland is created every day, and people make their settlements on sites where before stood only the great green desert. Only posterity can tell whether their labours have been a contribution to happiness or otherwise. The Peribonka area has since become part of civilisation and the turbulent waters of the same river now obediently work the turbines of a big electric plant. The lumber of the same forests has considerably increased in value, and for the exploitation of this lumber strong companies have been formed. The leaders of these companies certainly do not live together with the lumbermen in the woods; they live far away from the green frontier in comfortable cities, although they, in a sense, are the successors of the primitive pioneers. Year after year the enormous mass of logs floats down the river; they end up in cities as lumber for construction, or are used in far away mills to be transformed into paper for newsprint. The destroyed woods cannot retain rain and melting snow, and the topsoil is carried away; over large areas a brown, lonely desert landscape makes its appearance.

Maria Chapdelaine is the eldest of the six children of the family. The young men who saw her in the churchyard of Peribonka call her a beautiful, strong, and courageous girl.

Certainly she was not a type of city beauty, with modern hair-wave and make-up. She had simple, clear features; her blue eyes shone just as quietly as those of her mother and—without any doubt—just like her mother she will follow her future husband modestly, quietly and full of energy, without a murmur. She is at the right age for marriage, and all over the world this is not nearly such a sentimental situation amongst peasants as with townspeople. There are quite a few who would like to have her. The first is the only neighbour of the Chapdelaine's, a lumberman as the father is, but poorer; the second is the son of a peasant in Peribonka who has become a well-paid labourer in the United States, which he much prefers to the strenuous work in the forest. He has come home merely to sell his father's homestead.

Hemon portrays none of these persons in strong blacks and whites; the reader is expected to answer the many questions which the author leaves open. He does not portray the peasant's son as a tempter; he allows him, however, to tell Maria much about the pleasant side of life and the enjoyments of the big city as they actually exist. Maria, who has never seen such a city, has to use her imagination to compare these attractions with the hard life to which she has been accustomed in the woods. But the story has not yet progressed to the point where such a comparison is made vivid. Actually, her heart has already made its choice. She loves neither the industrious poor neighbour, nor the well-groomed young man from the big city; her heart belongs to the woodsman François Paradis.

Few novels portray with such tenderness and realism the scene as Hemon gives it to us. Far from the civilised world, in the midst of the woods, the two young people come face to face whilst picking blueberries, and they convey their love to each other without using words. The picture carries the fugitive sweetness of beauty and purity, and perhaps cannot even be fully appreciated by so-called cultured city people. Paradis promises to return to the young girl in the spring.

After the hard, unceasing labour during summer, fall comes

in this area like a surprise. Is it perhaps as a premonition of his own fate that Hemon wrote: 'Autumn is melancholy everywhere; filled with nostalgia and regret for everything that passes away, of apprehension for the things to come. But on Canadian soil autumn is more penetrating than anywhere else, more similar to the death of a human being whom the gods called before he had his full share of life.' Frost comes early this year, and the fall of snow in the Peribonka territory brings no joy; it is the white shroud that Nature gives to the earth. The calendar rapidly sheds its leaves: Christmas is near. Maria would have liked to attend midnight Mass in Peribonka; she feels many secret wishes in her heart which she would have liked to commit to the grace of heaven. She has no reason to doubt that her wishes will be granted; the secret happiness of her heart knows nothing of the dark powers which sometimes cruelly interfere between cup and lip. For a start, a snowstorm covers all the roads and prevents the journey. Nevertheless, Maria is intensely happy during Christmas Eve. With the simple, robust faith of the settlers of this country, she has found a way to secure the grace and the blessings of heaven. Devotedly she prays—a full thousand 'Ave Maria's' —and now she feels sure: next spring François will return and marry her. Outside, with unabated strength, the icy northern storm blows.

It is very difficult to test this novel critically for accomplishment and weakness. It may be due to the fact that Hemon made a mistake when selecting the instruments for his work. He took his pen but did not write—he painted. The full portrayal is visual and on top of this, every single detail is a separate picture. If looking for a specific name for the whole, again one is obliged to go outside the province of literary criticism; only one name seems warranted: a symphony. For there are works of art which can be read, seen and heard all at once.

At variance with the rough energy of normal days, New Year's Eve is quiet and intimate inside the log cabin lost in the snows. Mother Chapdelaine regrets that due to severe

weather no visitors can be expected. But late in the evening
the neighbour knocks at the door. His face rigid with frost
and snow, does not reflect a festive mood; he is the bearer of
tragic news. François Paradis had tried to travel from Lake
St. John, where he was lumbering, to the cabin of the Chapdelaine's in order to join them for the holiday. So far he has
not arrived and therefore must have lost his way in the woods.
On receiving the news all present realise that in this kind of
weather it means death—even to an experienced woodsman
like Paradis.

A literary dabbler would at this point have had Maria
collapse in tears. But Maria Chapdelaine is not solely a
creation of Hemon's fancy: he is in his novel a real craftsman
and does not present us with lifeless characters. Here he writes
more like a reporter than an artist, and he sees Nature and
mankind with unerring eyes; he reports truly and sincerely
what he sees. The people of this region are not accustomed to
showing their emotions openly; the effect of the blow remains
deep in the soul, and it is extremely rare that grief shows, even
in a few tears. If the blow has been very strong, even these
tears will dry up before they are visible.

Maria remains mute. A hand seems to have worked its way
down her throat to choke her; she feels the horrible pressure
of five fingers gripping her heart. Only after all the others are
sleeping does her grief become manifest, and everything of
which she had dreamed as future bliss collapse within. Despair
of this nature is without bounds. 'O, Jesus Christ, Thou who
extendest Thine arms to the forlorn and the unhappy, why
didst Thou lift him from the snow? Why, Holy Virgin, did not
Thy miracle support him, when he faltered for the last time?
And why, in the wide expanse of heaven, was there not one
single angel to show him the right road? Why . . . ?' The
eternal question, spared no bleeding heart on this earth. But
in the middle of such questions she stops, filled with fright.
Her simple, devoted heart fears they might be blasphemous,
because, in a simple soul like hers, the conception has not yet
died that there must be a logic of a higher order than available

to mankind. So she lifts her rosary again and prays for his poor soul: 'Holy Mary, full of mercy . . .'.

But life goes on, and so does the existence of the Chapdelaine family. Next to the attraction of the wealth of figures and colours, such as we may admire when looking at paintings of Pieter Breughel, the author is continually adding new and important scenes to his story. Now when her mother sighs and speaks of the disadvantages of their lonely life, with the ever present menace of catastrophes, it sounds so acceptable to Maria that she listens much more carefully than before. Her former wooer returns from the United States in the spring, and she sees the life there about which he tells her in quite a different light. She now looks upon the primitive wilderness and the murderous climate which have been the companions of the family for many years, with a feeling similar to hate. At one point in the story humour is interjected in the amusing incident of the arrival of a Parisian, a newcomer to the area, who on being asked how he likes the new country replies: 'it is a beautiful country, new and very large. . . . There are many flies in summer and the winters are difficult. But I assume that one becomes accustomed to it in time.'

It would be a good thing for Maria to get married, and the priest advises her to find herself a husband, but in revolving in her mind the possibility of marrying her neighbour the unbearable thought strikes her that it would mean remaining all her life tied down to exhausting labour, and in a sad and wild country. She cannot come to a decision, and spring is upon settlement. In accordance with the old saying of the peasants —'Once a hailstorm comes, the hail falls thick', her mother becomes ill. Her sufferings, and subsequent death and transfiguration, form the most touching and dramatic part of the work. It would be banal to write a commentary on such scenes, let the reader take the book in his hands and read it.

After these events the Chapdelaine house is even more lonely than before. Was it not the vengeance of the forest? Do not the roar of the early spring storms and the thunder of the nearby waterfall sound like a song of triumph of Nature over mankind? But no: the men who have settled here do not give up easily. The simple, self-sacrificing heart of Maria feels that in some way the emptiness left by her mother's departure has to be filled. She cannot desert her father and the younger children; she cannot let the modest homefire die. Instead of accepting the tempting offer from her friend in the United States, she decides to give her neighbour her promise of marriage.

Within a wild and grandiose frame, this novel is a masterly story of a simple heart. We do not put the book away without having obtained the definite feeling that in this rough country there must be more stout hearts who will say what Maria said, whenever the future or the welfare of Canada appears to be threatened: 'Three hundred years ago we arrived here to stay. . . . From ourselves and from our fates we have gained this understanding: to remain where we are, not to give in. And so we have maintained ourselves, so that perhaps after many centuries the world may say of us: these people form a nation that cannot die. This is why we must remain in the area where our ancestors fought the same battle and we must live as they lived and followed the mute command of their hearts—the same command we know and which our children shall know after us.'

With understandable enthusiasm, many readers have accepted Hemon's work as a wonderful portrayal of Canadian settler life. If they do it is against the wishes of the author, who clearly does not attempt to produce a representation of life of the whole of Canada or even of a particular province, but only of a tiny area north of Lake St. John defined with geographical exactness. Canada's area is larger than that of Europe, and offers so many different aspects of life that a full description would require many volumes of statistical and scientific study; it could never be encompassed in a work of art. Still, in a way, the reader's enthusiasm is justified. The stirrings of the soul as Hemon has portrayed them in his work, are to be found in all places where the simple hearts of these pioneers brave their fates and learn how to live in grief and happiness, merely doing their duty, with a strong love for the soil in which they will later rest from the burdens and diffi- culties of life. Much more than the frontiers of land and sea, these hearts form the Canadian nation. And in this sense, Hemon's novel is a truly national work.

Hemon finished the manuscript of 'Maria Chapdelaine' in Peribonka during his leisure hours. He left there in May 1913, and sent the work from Quebec to the 'Temps', which had already published his previous short novel 'Lizzie Blakestone'. Subsequently he went to Montreal and from there to the Province of Ontario. His travelling companion was apparently the young Canadian who had suggested emigration to Canada to him when he was in London.

The two young men found the travelling by rail too tedious, or perhaps too expensive. Upon arrival in the south-western part of Ontario they decided to continue the trip as a walking tour. For long stretches they walked along the railway line of the Canadian Pacific, as there was no other road through the impenetrable forests. There were certainly no highways at that time. It will never be known what problems so engrossed them that they did not hear an oncoming express-train, and were killed the next moment.

Even if, confronted with this all too sudden end of two young lives, we cover our faces, we have the consolation that their passing away took place before they were old enough to pass through many valleys of suffering. There existence was from light to light. Their death took place on the 8th of July, 1913, near the railway station of Chapleau. Meanwhile the 'Temps' had accepted Hemon's novel, and their letter of confirmation was on the way to him. The letter was returned to the publishers stamped 'Deceased'. 'Maria Chapdelaine' appeared for the first time in the 'Temps' in 1914, and was subsequently edited in book form in Montreal in 1915. Grate- fully, Canada dedicated a memorial tomb to Hemon, and a statue in Peribonka. A little lake near this village was called after him, and a second one after his famous work 'Maria Chapdelaine'.

Susanna Moodie

Investigate our early literature we must, regardless of the literary value we are predisposed to allow it—investigate it so that we may come to know ourselves, if for no other reason.

How can we better find ourselves, as individuals and as a people, than by studying the writings of the past, and by submitting ourselves to the historical ethos preserved best of all in literature, that certain preservative of values and attitudes? How, indeed, can we know ourselves at all without revisiting the beginnings, let alone know the world, know nations, peoples, policies of wisdom and folly? But more than this, more than the knowledge of ourselves, although all one in the process, is the beginning of literature in our own time. For without the past can we write the present? How can we expect to produce literature (we do not speak here of the other arts, yet it applies equally to them) unless we know, actually live into, the minds of our older writers, in order to learn their problems, how they overcame them or why they failed to overcome them. Without the study of our past authors—not the mere schoolbook learning, but the heart-and-mind-given attention —we cannot create a literature of and for our own time. For only as our forbears became conscious of themselves can we become conscious of ourselves, since they are our past and therefore our present, and not only our national but also our individual and anthropological past and present. Only then, living on direct continuity with the life of many before us, can we become psychologically instinct with the language power and the matter of our own time, knowing truly what we are. Let us make no mistake about it: we do not find ourselves except through our forbears, and we cannot produce a literature without finding ourselves.

Half of a century ago, Pelham Edgar wrote the following comment on English-Canadian literature up to the twentieth century: 'Other countries have a progressive tradition and a harmonious evolution little interrupted by artificial considerations; whereas, with us, literature is compelled to be almost completely artifice'. Once accept the vapid abstractions, and the general idea is seen to be sound enough. Furthermore, the ease with which Canadians may acquire satisfying foreign products of art, especially due to high pressure salesmanship from south of the border; the severe competition offered to the young Canadian writer by those of other countries of an established cultural tradition; the absence of a professional class of artists at all comparable in number, variety of talent, and spiritual stature, which could offer technical and commercial advice if nothing else; the enormous extent and correspondingly tiny population of the country, which makes satisfactory contact between centres of culture very difficult; the reactionary caution of some Canadian publishers when confronted with Canadian writing; the small Canadian market—comprising the southern neighbour—and the consequent preference of publishers for best-sellers of any country; the very spirit of defeatism engendered by a knowledge of such factors: all work against the production of a literature that can take its place with the best of any country.

A hundred years ago, however, a Canadian author was faced with all these difficulties and more. The subject of this study, Mrs. Moodie, had to put up with the additional factor of absolute frontier conditions, at least during her first years in Canada. This meant endless physical labour for necessities; lack of time, lack of cultivated audience; lack of printing facilities, lack of a unitive culture; heart-sickness destructive of the creative urge; and perhaps most important of all, the absence of even a 'shadowy outline' of the genuine Canadian type so essential to the art of the Canadian novelist, a type at that time indistinguishable from recent emigrants from Europe and the United States.

With all these problems Mrs. Moodie coped successfully, and through the writing of one book, 'Roughing it in the Bush, or Life in Canada', earned herself a certain position in any critical history of Canadian literature that may come to be written. Susanna Moodie was born in Bungay, Suffolk, on December 6th, 1803, the youngest daughter of Thomas Strickland, of Reydon Hall, and one of five sisters and a brother all authors and all destined to longevity of life if not of fame. Agnes Strickland is still known for her popular 'Lives of the Queens of England' written in co-authorship with her sister Elizabeth. Catherine Parr was the instigator of the flood of writing turned out by the family, through the popular success of her first volume of children's stories published at an early age in 1818, two years after her father's death. Authorship was encouraged by the children's guardian, and all sisters produced voluminously, in the fashion of Victorian lady writers of their time; only the single son, Samuel, failed to maintain production by publishing one work.

Catherine, later Mrs. Traill, emigrated to Canada the same year as her sister marrying a lieutenant of the 21st Royal Scots Fusiliers, also John Moodie's unit. She produced many volumes on Canadian life, and was especially talented in the field of plant life; her writings on Canadian flora and fauna, the result of a fine herbarium collected over many years—a not unusual object of study for educated Canadians of the period—appeared after her husband's death. She and her husband lived in a log cabin for seven years, and anticipating Susanna, she recorded the vicissitudes of life there for a wide English and Canadian audience, perhaps most effectively in 'The Backwoods of Canada' published in 1835. This and the later 'Female Emigrants Guide' drew many newcomers to the colony. She wrote as well for a number of periodicals, and was the first writer of animal stories in Canada.

Samuel Strickland came to Canada as early as 1825. In 1828 he was engaged by the eminent founder of cities and director of the Canada Company, John Galt, to superintend a development in the Huron Tract, and afterwards settled on a farm at Lakefield in Upper Canada. He served in the militia during the Rebellion, retired with the rank of colonel, and became Justice of the Peace. In 1853 he published 'Twenty-seven Years in Canada West', a book still worth reading for the vivid picture it gives of colonial life at that time. The nine children had an unusual upbringing due to their father's liberal ideas on education, and spent a happy childhood in an agricultural village in the valley of Waveney. They were not encouraged to play with the village children, but despite this privation they were content, reading in the well-stocked home library, enacting Shakespeare, poring over history. Their paternal grandmother had been descended from the Penderell who saved the life of Charles II in the oak tree of Boscobel, while the father's first wife had been the grand-niece of Isaac Newton. Therefore among the books read there by Susanna was Newton's copy of Pope's translation of the 'Iliad', together with Hornbeck's 'Divine Morality', and Locke's 'Essay on the Human Understanding'.

In 1831, the year that Michael Faraday discovered the induction of electric currents, that saw the publishing of Stendhal's 'Le Rouge et le Noir' and the death of Georg Hegel, a year of eminent events in science, philosophy and literature, Susanna published her first book 'Enthusiasm, and other Poems'. It was dedicated to the reformer-poet James Montgomery, and reflects the same kind of simple romantic sensibility. She wrote with apparent ease, and at times her blank verse faintly echoes Wordsworth. There are no personal love poems—she is fond of declaring herself 'void of passion's dross'—which leads us to suspect that she had not yet met her future husband, although it was to take place the same year. The volume contains little for comment. Her object was the usual one of such talented ladies as herself: to versify conventional subjects—fame, the deluge, war—and to write occasional poems as exercises on subjects considered poetically apt. She had a certain facility with language and metre, but although she invoked inspiration there is nothing but obvious imagery and the pious sentiment of orthodoxy. Today one writes prose with some competence; at that time both to read poetry continually and to write it with ease were the expected accomplishment of almost any educated young person.

As the distinction of the socially accomplished, poetry was considered to be a business of felicitous metre and perfect rhymes; the set task was to fit one's thought into verse and to embroider it with decorous figurative language. James Montgomery had done so—although with greater pietistic favour and strength of image than his follower—and Susanna Strickland would do likewise. Add to this the powerful urge to didacticism, and we have the poetic which motivated Mrs. Moodie's verse even in Canada. John Dunbar Moodie, of Melsetter in the Orkney Islands, was in many respects a remarkable man. After considerable army service he spent about twelve years in residence near his brother's home in South Africa on a farm of his own. His father had been a major and his brother rose through the civil service to a magistracy. The latter was intensely active over the racial problem, and doubtless communicated his enthusiasm through John to Susanna to add to her already keen humanitarian sympathies with the victims of slavery anywhere in the world. One of her first poems had dealt with West Indian slavery, at least partly in imitation of Montgomery's 'The West Indies', while a later story and polemical passages in 'Roughing it in the Bush' reflect her passion on the subject at a time when England was debating the 1833 abolition bill, and John Greenleaf Whittier '. . . left the Muses haunt to turn the crank of an opinion mill' in favour of the slaves.

Lieutenant Moodie met his future wife at the London home of a mutual literary friend—he was also an author, having published an account of 'Ten Years in South Africa'—and they were married within a few weeks. He tried to persuade his wife to return with him to South Africa, to which he was deeply attached and where he owned a fine property. She adamantly refused, however, largely due to fear of wild animals, and when he remonstrated she produced his account of exaggerated adventure to prove her point. The first volume of Mrs. Moodie's which concerns us is the autobiographical 'Flora Lindsay', not published until 1854, but detailing the early marriage, the poverty of a half-pay officer, the arrival of the first child, and for her the frightening decision to emigrate to Canada. They set sail in a ship of 180 tons from Port Leith, Scotland, and after a voyage of nine weeks made their first stop off 'Grosse Isle' below Quebec. Once within the St. Lawrence the writing quickens under the stimulus of the natural wonders on either side of the river, and the novel concludes with descriptions of a thunderstorm and of the mountains, passages displaying acute observation and strong feeling: 'The previous day had been dark and stormy; and a heavy fog had concealed the mountain chain, which forms the stupendous background to this sublime view, entirely from our sight. As the clouds rolled away from their grey, bald brows, and cast into denser shadow the vast forest belt that girdled them round, they loomed out like mighty giants—Titans of the earth, in all their rugged and awful beauty—a thrill of wonder and a delight pervaded my mind. The spectacle floated dimly on my sight—my eyes were blinded with tears—blinded with the excess of beauty, I turned to the right and to the left, I looked up and down the glorious river; never had I beheld so many striking objects blended into one mighty whole. Nature had lavished all her noblest features in producing that enchanting scene.' It was autumn, and this most attractive and delightful season of the year evokes a typical Canadian tribute, the love of autumn being as characteristic of a Canadian as is his detestation of the dismal weeks of spring. One previous Canadian novelist, Mrs. Francis Brooke, in two novels written during the third quarter of the eighteenth century, had waxed equally if more exotically enthusiastic over the Canadian scene, where 'one sees not only the beautiful but the great sublime to an amazing degree'.

The famous 'Roughing it' takes up the story where 'Flora Lindsay' had left it, with its opening sentence: 'The dreadful cholera was depopulating Quebec and Montreal, when our ship cast anchor off Grosse Isle, on the 30th of August, 1832, and we were boarded a few minutes after by the health-officers'. Such was their foreboding first contact with a land whose wilderness and primitive customs were to be the occasion of recurrent heart-break and nostalgic lamentation until after the Rebellion. After a delay of some days the ship moved on up the St. Lawrence to Quebec, the sight of which in all its grandeur stirred the depths of her romantic sensibility, and evoked one of her most intelligently emotional passages of writing: 'Nature has lavished all her grandest elements to form this astonishing panorama. There frowns the cloud-capped mountain, and below, the cataract foams and thunders; wood, and rock, and river combine to lend their aid in making the picture perfect, and worthy of its Divine Originator. The precipitous bank upon which the city lies piled, reflected in the still deep waters at its base, greatly enhances the romantic beauty of the situation. The mellow and serene glow of the autumnal day harmonised so perfectly with the solemn grandeur of the scene around me, and sank so silently and deeply into my soul, that my spirit fell prostrate before it.' They proceeded by land from Montreal to the town of Cobourg on Lake Ontario, which on their arrival comprised a single long street parallel with the lake, with neat, painted wooden houses on either side. At that time it was a clearing house for land-jobbers and incoming settlers to the Trent valley. Immediately beyond could be seen farms stretching for some miles into the backwoods, and the overriding sensation of the Moodies was one of being hemmed in by a limitless, chaotic but ruthless green monster. They purchased an already cleared farm eight miles from Cobourg for 300 livres sterling shortly after their arrival, and from that moment one misery succeeded another.

Mrs. Moodie describes the pathetically ordered removal to the farm on a stormy October day. Apparently no one had thought it necessary to examine the place thoroughly, and on arrival they discovered that they were destined to inhabit a small single-room cabin minus door and window-glass, having been formerly persuaded by a callous land-jobber to accept it until the inefficient tenants of the farmhouse should decide to move out. It was actually the following June before they got possession of their farmhouse, then little cleaner than a pigsty, after having moved once again to an even smaller shack. Incidents of high interest, however, crowd the intervening chapters, one of the most graphic being her account of 'borrowing', a monstrous social evil at the time whereby the irresponsible gradually stripped the indulgent and generous of belongings while technically not violating the law. Especially adept at this practice were debased 'Yankee' emigrants, who played on the English reserve and suspension of disbelief culti- vated by the newcomers as an act of faith in the great potential of the young country. The pilferers drew down on their heads, however, the bitter execration of one whom they had no doubt labelled as 'unmitigated sucker', and through her exposure of their ways suffered a gradual obliteration.

Mrs. Moodie uses these 'Yankees', in fact, to demonstrate one of the major points of her social theory, i.e., that the social contract must rightly lead to the establishment of stratification according to innate temperamental and intellectual differ- ences. Despite her romanticism, the author's political pre- possessions were too deeply ingrained to permit her support of what appeared to her as anarchic republicanism. Both she and her husband, however, took care to distinguish between the majority of American republicans who allowed the distinction founded on cultivated natural gifts and those few who would interpret the new continental principles as licence for irrespon- sibility. It was when subject to the continuous proximity, depredations, and insults of such low types that Mrs. Moodie wrote: 'At that period my love for Canada was a feeling very nearby allied to that which the condemned criminal enter- tains for his cell—his only hope of escape being through the portals of the grave'. With this we might immediately contrast a typical statement from the novel 'Flora Lindsay' represent- ing her later feelings: 'Thank God I am the denizen of a free land; a land of beauty and progression. A land unpollited by the groans of starving millions. A land which opens her fostering arms to receive and restore to his long lost birthright, the trampled and abused child of poverty.' Another aspect of optimistic feelings running throughout her work, and alternating with despondency even during the early years, is the clear affirmation of a belief in Canada's great future. Such a statement is significantly placed at the front of 'Roughing it in the Bush', in a poem entitled 'Canada':

> 'Canada, the blest—the free!
> With prophetic glance, I see
> Visions of thy future glory,
> Giving to the world's great story
> A page, with mighty meaning fraught,
> That asks a wider range of thought.
> Borne onward on the wings of time,
> I trace thy future course sublime;
> And feel my anxious lot grow bright,
> While musing on the glorious sight;—
> My heart rejoicing bounds with glee
> To hail thy noble destiny.'

A further delightful expression of joy in the new country is the well-known 'Sleigh-Bells', written about this time while awaiting her husband's return to the shanty. It was sung in many versions and set to music in the United States, and is perhaps her best known song and deservedly famous, since it skilfully catches the Canadian winter scene, not only of those early frontier days but also of the backwoods today:

> ''Tis merry to hear, at evening time,
> By the blazing hearth the sleigh-bell's chime;
> To know the bounding steeds bring near
> The loved one to our bosom dear.
> Ah, lightly we spring the fire to raise,
> Till the rafters glow with the ruddy blaze;
> These merry sleigh-bells, our hearths keep time
> Responsive to their fairy chime.

Ding-dong, ding-dong, o'er vale and hill
Their welcome notes are trembling still.'

Once in possession of farm and farmhouse, the latter cleared
of vermin and of a dead skunk purposely left behind in a
cupboard by the previous tenants, and the business of planting
upon them, Mr. Moodie was persuaded to settle his farm out
in shares to a tried farmer. Unfortunately they were mercilessly gulled once more, although it must be said that their at
times incredible impracticality—Mrs. Moodie's refusal at that
time to perform certain household tasks, for example—invited
disaster.

Such a disability, as a matter of fact, leads us to her weakness as the author of 'Roughing it in the Bush'. Despite her
tolerance and perseverance in the face of countless disappointments, and those largely stemming from the contrast between
a comparatively barbarous way of life and the ordered social
pattern from which she had removed, she was too much the
narrow provincial gentlewoman of early nineteenth-century
England. She owned too many prejudices to record her history
of the new undertaking with the fully impartial eye and deeply
discerning sensibility necessary to fix a perpetual memorial of
this new kind of social experiment. To put it quite simply, she
lacked the vision to glean all the relevant particulars, the
greater majority she did observe having obvious reference to
the amenities of her class in England. Such commentary is not
intended to frighten readers away from what is obviously one
of the better works of Canadian literature of the nineteenth
century; it is intended, however, as an introduction to the
serious treatment of Canadian writing, an attempt to regard
Canadian authorship with no gentler or less firm an eye than
one would allow any other work of art. If we are going to
hope for a literature in this country we must not shy away
from serious criticism of that which we already have, whether
for the feeble fear of inhibiting present growth or for any other
reason.

The advantages of deciding on one's genre before writing

are illustrated by the failure of 'Roughing it in the Bush' to be any of history, memoir, autobiography, travel book, anthropology or sociology. It is not the first because of the omission of many necessary items—a discussion of political issues, for example; as anthropology or sociology it lacks the wide and painstaking scientific treatment of details, and a full enough view of cultural phenomena—as the chapter on the Indians shows. It is not autobiography because it too often deviates into incidental sketches to the forfeit of great parts of her own story, and there is little attempt at self-analysis of mental and emotional character. And there is not enough travelling done for a travel book. So far, these are not defects, since they were not part of Mrs. Moodie's intention; we can take it that if she had any genre specifically in mind it was that of a memoir.

It comes closest, in fact, to a memoir, a sketch of events without a pressing need for their consistent examination from certain specific points of view other than that of the idiosyncracy of the author. Yet for one thing, it lacks the consistent literary style of a memoir, both in the intrusion of her husband's two chapters, and in the absence of a highly individualised approach to events. One suspects that she lacked the literary force of personality necessary to colour all she saw with her own human light; it is coloured instead with the light of a unit—an exceptional one, to be sure—of a social class. The literary quality of the work as a whole is affected by these disadvantages: it is a highly competent piece of realistic writing—except where her educated sense of propriety skirts certain essential aspects of the life she is observing—set off by a few powerful passages of romantic nature description. Her talent was much less for analytic enquiry than for surface description, yet even the latter loses power to some extent through a lack of form. All writing is, or should be initiated for some purpose, and purpose demands form. Mrs. Moodie, by compounding a series of chronologically arranged sketches, sacrifices through lack of structural integration any marked literary distinction. There is a psychological reason for this, for her domestic memoir divides attention between the mind of a middle-class English gentlewoman of that time, and the conditions of life in the colony. She has been caught between the two stools of realistic reportage of settler life and psychological self-portraiture, based in this case on a radical change in the individual due to altered environment. Not that she had any idea of the latter as a literary purpose for her work: did she not use an injunction to realism as a motto for the book: 'I sketch from Nature, and the picture's true'—and, in 'Life in the Clearings', defend novel writing on realistic and didactic grounds?

But the divided treatment is there, to add to the charm of a literary curiosity and to detract from the formal perfection. We must also remember her declared intention in writing the book: to deter 'well-educated people, about to settle in this colony, from entering upon a life for which they were totally unfitted by their previous pursuits and habits'. Fortunately Mrs. Moodie was not completely successful in this latter respect, having underestimated the hunger of the spirit for personal freedom and a 'second chance'; and she had allowed that a judicious choice of location (i.e. not in the backwoods) could lead to material and social blessings. And finally, as in any question of genre, we must take into consideration her model, Mrs. Traill's 'The Backwoods of Canada'. She scores Canadian foibles with a keen phrase and a well-merited contempt, especially when momentarily forgetful of her grievance that inferiors show her too little respect. There is a sharp neo-classic tang and neat compactness about many of her pronouncements, that is reminiscent of Haliburton as on the vanity of dress in the colony: 'The aristocracy of wealth is bad enough; but the aristocracy of dress is perfectly contemptible. Could Raphael visit Canada in rags, he would be nothing in their eyes beyond a common sign painter.' The contrast is still observable between England and Canada in this respect, and is possibly less due to economic austerity in the former country than to the Canadian desire for external compensation for a feeling of cultural insecurity. The same skill appears in passages on the pretensions of the illiterate; the disparagement of the arts; the large annual parties; the lack of courtesy; the boldness of young Canadian women, their poverty of conversation, and their beauty: 'Yet they have abilities, excellent practical abilities, which, with a little mental culture, would render them intellectual and charming companions. At present, too many of these truly lovely girls remind one of choice flowers half buried in weeds.'

But to return to the story of economic tribulation, we find that tempted by the rich gains obtainable in land speculation, and misled to believe that the heavy immigration of 1832 into the Trent district would continue, Mr. Moodie joined the forces of that species of gambler willing to trade on pure Chance. They were unhappy in their neighbours as before mentioned, and on being coaxed by Mrs. Moodie's brother Samuel and sister Catherine to join their settlement forty miles north, they used a recent legacy of 700 livres to add three hundred uncleared acres to the sixty-six obtained for them by Samuel. The whole transaction proved to be sheer folly for several reasons, since they knew nothing about living and working conditions in the backwoods, the hoped-for immigrants turned from the district due to a cholera epidemic and chance movement elsewhere, and a government development of the Trent valley which would have raised the property value was dropped. The land was sold fifteen years later for less than the purchase price. But that was not the end of the madness. A sly speculator talked Moody into selling his half-pay army commission to him for shares in a steamer to traffic on Lake Ontario. The ship was built, but rival interests at York prevented the Cobourg investors from realising any profits on the shipping. All this on top of the move to the wilderness in order to escape neighbourly rapacity was not exactly a happy intimation of the next phase.

The party crossed the Otonabee River under moonlight on their way to the lot eleven miles beyond Peterborough, and despite all misfortune Mrs. Moodie was stimulated, as always, by the natural beauty of the scene, to write one of her most powerful descriptions, one which places her at the time as much closer to Romantic than Neoromantic sympathies: 'Even while the rocky banks are coated with ice, and the frost-king suspends from every twig and branch the most beautiful and fantastic crystals, the black waters rush foaming along, a thick steam rising constantly above the rapids, as from a boiling pot. The shores vibrate and tremble beneath the force of the impetuous flood, as it whirls round cedar-crowned islands and opposing rocks. The most renowned of our English rivers dwindle into little muddy rills when compared with the sublimity of the Canadian waters. No language can adequately express the solemn grandeur of her lake and river scenery; the glorious islands that float, like visions from fairy land, upon the bosom of these azure mirrors of her cloudless skies. The rocky shores are crowned with the cedar, the birch, the alder, and soft maple, that dip their long tresses in the pure stream; from every crevice on the limestone the hare-bell and Canadian rose wave their graceful blossoms.' There she and her two children, a second girl having been born on the farm, lived with her sister Catherine until their log cabin on the nearby shores of a beautiful lake was completed. The cabin was of a quite respectable size—thirty-six by thirty-two feet, with four rooms—and far better than average. Now for a few weeks they enjoyed 'halcyon' days fishing, shooting, canoeing, and becoming more reconciled to their lot than previously owing to the sheer beauty of their surroundings. They became friendly with the Chippewa Indians of the district, and a picturesque section of the account is devoted to their ways.

Within a year twenty acres about the house had been cleared, the fallow fired, and three logging bees held in order to ready the land for crops. It was at this time that Mrs. Moodie was attacked by the ague during the birth of her third child, their first son, but fortunately recovered and continued to make those lifelike, impressionistic sketches of the pioneers she met, and descriptions of the wild country about her, which are the highlights of her writing. During the summer of 1835 an exceptional period of rain completely ruined their wheat crop, and once more was initiated a series of misfortunes that resulted in the total destitution of the Moodies. Their steamboat stock paid nothing, they owed money for the land clearance, fire half destroyed the cabin and for food they were forced to rely upon roots, fish and the results of hunting. But just at that time, in accordance with Mrs. Moodie's belief in the benevolence of divine providence towards the worthy, on December 4th, 1837, they received news of the siege of Toronto by rebel forces. The Rebellion was in progress, and John Moody, with little or no knowledge of the causes at stake for Reform party or Family Compact, like a true-blue Britisher left the following day to put down the rebels. Within a week he was back, but by January had received a captaincy and been posted to Point Abino on Lake Erie, since there was a danger of incursions across the border by rebels stirred up by Mackenzie. Mrs. Moodie was left alone with the children and one servant to cope with the farm as best she could and to write stirring Neo-Loyalist verses in support of the government. These received wide distribution and acclaim throughout the colony, although they are of little literary interest today with their bombastic aggrandising of event and sentiment. It was possibly the popularity of these verses in the Canadas that led Mr. Lovell, the editor of the newly-founded Montreal magazine, the 'Literary Garland', to ask Mrs. Moodie for articles, poems, and stories. Her first payment was twenty dollars, the result of writing through the night by the light of candles made from rags dipped in pork lard. She also discovered an art of painting birds and butterflies on a certain kind of sugar-maple fungi, and with the proceeds from sales to officers she was able to buy shoes for the children.

From this time dates the large contribution Susanna Moodie made to the artistic life of the colony. There can be little doubt that the settlement of the Stricklands in Upper Canada considerably hastened due appreciation of the arts. By contributing to the 'Literary Garland', which also published work by other noted authors such as C. P. Dunlop and Charles Sangster, the sisters helped to foster if not initiate the romantic movement in Canadian literature. During this time two other periodicals had made brief appearances in Upper Canada, but unlike certain contemporary French-Canadian magazines, failed almost immediately for want of support. The first, the 'Canadian Literary Magazine' of Toronto, lasted three numbers, while its contemporary the 'Canadian Magazine', did not reach a third issue. By December, 1851, the 'Literary Garland' had been done to death by the competition of the American 'Harper's Magazine' and the 'International', both able to offer finer literary fare more cheaply. In the forties at last two other ventures were hopefully begun, but both failed within the year. The Moodies themselves made an effort in the joint editorship of an inexpensive monthly, the 'Victoria Magazine', published in Belleville. The subscription list totalled the surprising number of eight hundred, with all the annual five shilling fees pain in advance; but the failure of its proprietor put an end to its circulation. All the evidence, however, points to the fact that Canadian readers up to and beyond the time of Confederation were more interested in political articles in newspapers than in romances, even though Mrs. Moodie should have wondered that the striking natural prospects of Canada did not inspire an imaginative national literature of merit. She found, in deed, that most native-born authors whom she and her husband so earnestly wished to publish, failed to produce work suitable for their periodical, and they put it down to the ascendancy of the practical over the imaginative in Canada. John Bourinot came to much the same conclusion in 1893: 'Dollard, and the Lady of Fort la Tour are themes which we do not find in Prosaic Ontario, whose history is only a century old—a history of stern materialism as a rule, rarely picturesque or romantic, and hardly even heroic except in some episodes of the war of 1812—though their deeds have never yet been adequately told in poem or prose'. Bourinot held a narrow conception of the 'heroic', but the 'stern materialism' he observed was one with the 'practical' bent noted by Mrs. Moodie. For the time being, however,

Canadian readers showed a healthy intuition in their political preoccupations. Political polemic is bound to run high during a time of settlement and conflict between reactionary and reform elements—here we must remember that Canada was then fighting for its very political life—and no other method of circulation is as satisfactory for this purpose as the newspaper; the rise of journalism on a large scale coincided with the rise of English party government during the eighteenth century. In Canada too, the polemic although vigorous to the point of distasteful crudity at times, was much more vital than any imaginative literature on display in the available periodicals; it is little wonder, then, that the latter were largely disregarded.

But we have gone ahead of our story, and must now return to the spring of 1838. On hearing that her husband stood to be discharged, yet still faced with what seemed to be an immovable mountain of debt, Mrs. Moodie wrote to Sir George Arthur, the Lieutenant-Governor, clearly stating their position and asking that her husband be kept on in army service. A few days after the birth of her third son Captain Moodie received an army appointment as paymaster, and it was at the conclusion of this service that he became sheriff of Victoria County (now Hastings) a position he was to hold until 1863—and the family moved to Belleville. The long years of privation were over. The 1857 edition of 'Roughing it in the Bush' contains an excellent appended account by Sheriff Moodie of the social and economic status of Belleville for the information of future emigrants. He commences by attesting to the realism of his wife's sketches, and goes on to write a stirring eulogy of the land of his adoption. He attributes the 'indomitable energy of character' and general resourcefulness of the new settler to the exacting environmental demands: 'Nature looks sternly on him, and in order to preserve his own existence he must conquer Nature, as it were, by his perseverance and ingenuity'; he also contends that for similar reasons Canadian farmers 'are certainly far superior in general intelligence' to the British yeoman, and possess minds 'better stocked with ideas'. Such statements are doubtless intended to balance the impression given by Mrs. Moodie's conclusion to the first edition: 'If these sketches should prove the means of deterring one family from sinking their property, and shipwrecking all their hopes, by going to reside in the backwoods of Canada, I shall consider myself amply repaid for revealing the secrets of the prisonhouse, and feel that I have not toiled and suffered in the wilderness in vain'. As a concomitant of this unavoidable struggle which Sheriff Moodie had himself undergone, he argues—while denying any political intent in his pages—that the creation of an aristocracy under such conditions would have been futile, and that the government must of necessity be republican; he attempts to depict the uselessness of government by Compact, and to show the misfortune of exclusively bestowing political office on Loyalist and Tory. The whole essay of this liberal-minded man is worth reading.

Belleville, he tells us, had originally been a reserve for Mississagua Indians, and only in 1816 had it been laid out as a village containing a handful of white traders. Once the fringing forest had been cleared it began to grow in importance until in 1839 when the District of Victoria was set up, Belleville had 1,500 inhabitants, increasing within a decade to 4,000. Even at that time it was exporting 52,000 livres worth of goods to the United States, with a favourable trade balance of 33,000 livres. This happy advantage was largely due to Belleville's enviable situation on the Moira River where it empties into the Bay of Quinté, resulting in a heavy port business and lumber trade, and the establishment of many industries, especially tailoring and shoe-manufacturing. And as an indication of cultural conditions during the Moodies' time, for the twelve years preceding 1857 pianos in the town increased from five to a hundred, and there were five schools, four of them free. That in brief is the incomparably more congenial background for Mrs. Moodie's later years until moving to Toronto on her husband's death in 1869, and explains the significant alteration in tone of her next and last volume descriptive of the country, 'Life in the Clearings versus the Bush'. Its chapters, as well as those of 'Roughing it . . .', had first appeared in the 'Literary Garland', but represented the Belleville period of her life. This volume was purposely written to picture 'the present state of society in the colony, and to point out its increasing prosperity and commercial advantages'. 'Roughing it' had sufficiently counteracted the false stories which had been circulated in Britain to encourage emigration to Canada, and the new book was much lighter in tone, if not as stirring as that dealing with isolated bush life. It deals with the period when Mrs. Moodie was able to regard herself as a Canadian by adoption, 'the happy mother of Canadian children, rejoicing in the warmth and hospitality of a Canadian home'.

But 'Life in the Clearings' is not the book that 'Roughing it . . .' was, and the explanation is to be found in the given degree of talent and in the early upbringing of the author. There were several long and very bad novels which followed, none of them readable today, although unfortunately parts of them were relished by readers of the 'Literary Garland'. Mrs. Moodie is, in fact, illustrative of a paradox obtaining in many writers of her day: the combination of the pious didactic wish to 'sketch from Nature' with a patent unreality of sentiment. It runs through all her work in varying degrees, and with the exception of her writings on Canada the unreality of senti-ment vitiates almost everything she wrote. In those two works, however, and especially in the earlier, we can only suppose that the soul-shaking shock of adverse and primitive conditions such as drove her to night-long tears over an extended period, cracked her sheltered middle-class veneer and sentimentality to such an extent that, in combination with sensitive nature appreciation under ideal conditions, realty was directly apprehended. Aware that serious criticisms had been levelled at her by various newspaper critics for her adverse account of settler life in 'Roughing it', she reasserted her realistic purpose and what had been her intention there, to uphold the idea of a 'Commonwealth of intellect' while affirming that equality of station is an unreal dream. She managed, too, to make a finally reiterated point of desired British sovereignty for Canada. These were typical views held by the average, enlightened, formerly middle-class British settler in the Canadas, and it is this very representativeness of Mrs. Moodie's work that constitutes one of its important values.

The adherence to Britain up to the end of the nineteenth century and after, must be seen in its true light before we can justly evaluate the literary derivation from that quarter. Throughout the century, not discounting post-Confederation years, even the most nationalistic Canadians experienced moments of despair over the ability of Canada to hold her own on the continent in the face of annexationist fervour, national hatred, political party differences, British indifference, economic instability, commercial graft, educational controversy, trade disagreements, and loss after loss of land, capital, and prestige in treaty decisions.

It was in the face of such disillusionment over the future of the Canadian nation that some of the finest patriotic verse was composed: by the French-Canadian with usually an autonomous and regional note; by the English-Canadian, usually with tireless emphasis on the advantages of maintaining close ties with the Empire. Crémazie and Fréchette were amongst the French-Canadian nationalist poets, while Joseph Howe's 'Flag of Old England' is typical of English-Canadian sentiment in Susanna Moodie's time. Also Mrs. Moodie was a tireles supporter of Imperial sovereignty, and it was doubtless well nourished through the desperate years of homesickness when she wrote so many of the 'exile' poems of 'Roughing it in the Bush'. Subtitled 'A Canadian Song', and set to music by her flautist husband, the following must represent the many scattered throughout her work voicing the painful nostalgia of those who, at least during their early years on the land, could only regard themselves as unwilling exiles:

> 'Oh! can you leave your native land
> An exile's bride to be;
> Your mother's home, and cheerful hearth

To tempt the main with me;
Across the wide and stormy sea
To trace our foaming track,
And know the wave that bears us on
Will ne'er convey us back?
And can you in Canadian woods
With me the harvest bind,
Nor feel one lingering, sad regret
For all you leave behind?'

That is the authentic note of the pre-Confederation exile, a ballad note, simple, stark, yearning, possessing a quiet plaintive beauty of its own only possible in a direct transcription of experience. Reminiscence is a dominant characteristic of nineteenth century Canadian literature to Confederation; as there was little social integration of groups or even families, so their lives were fragmentary and they therefore nostalgically orientated themselves towards an earlier period of wholeness in the home country. Mrs. Moodie's Canadian writing is in the main stream of this tradition, but she enriches that tradition—and this is her considerable additional strength—in her loving depiction of the Canadian scene, character, and way of life.

Charles Gill

Sorel is a small industrial town and in some ways a typical matter-of-fact community of the New World. It is located at a spot where the clear Richelieu River mixes in a foaming andante with the darker and mightier St. Lawrence. The immense span of the sky arches impressively over the wide, majestic waters. If they were in Europe, such a combination of streams—like that of the Rhine and the Danube—would give birth to countless sagas and old historical reminiscences. The poetic appeal of the spot is strong, but the number of sagas is limited; it is only a few centuries ago that the first European settlers came to live in its neighbourhood. The romantic landscape makes many of the visitors wonder why, precisely, this place developed into a hive of industrial activity, full of noise and a people who seem never to have a moment to spare. Looking at the people of Sorel of today you would not get the impression that they could ever have given such a problem any thought. Perhaps the mighty stream took its revenge for this lack of contemplation; Sorel became the birth-place of an individual different in kind from its manufacturers and merchants, and from all those who want to make there a fortune. This man was a poet simply, and also a bohemian, not excessively remarkable in itself, if he had not been the first true bard of the St. Lawrence.

Charles Ignace Adelard Gill, born in Sorel on the 31st of October 1871, was the son of the well-to-do lawyer Charles Gill and his wife Delphira, born Senecal, who came from a wealthy and influential French-Canadian family. It was just in this year that old France had lost together with a bitter war the fame of an imperial grandeur as well as relinquished the romance surrounding its last Emperor. The history of the Gill family is interesting at many points. They were descended from the Scotch, who had immigrated to the State of Massachusetts in the United States in the seventeenth century and from there went to Canada. Towards the end of that century a young lad, Samuel Gill, was kidnapped by the Abonaki Indians during a surprise attack, and up to this date you will find a number of families called Gill amongst these Indians. There are no known blood-ties between Charles Gill and Indian women, but it is a fact that Charles is a descendant of Samuel Gill. The Gill's, on immigrating to Canada at an early date, took up life amongst the French-Canadians, and therefore must be accepted as such over several centuries. On comparing photographs of Gill and his grandfather Senecal, it is obvious that Charles is more like his French grandfather than like the Gill family.

Charles lived at his parents home in Sorel until he was nine years of age, spending his vacations with his grandparents, the Senecal's, on their beautiful country estate in Pierreville. He was well developed physically, strong and good looking, but unfortunately something seemed to be amiss in his inner life. At home, free from all material worries, it was not rare that the youth, who had a great affection for his older sister, became dreamy and showed signs of an excessively romantic disposition. Above all else he liked literature, and learned to read and write at an early age. Apart from this, he caused his parents a great deal of worry; he was disobedient, capricious and generally a difficult boy. Several primary schools in Sorel, and some secondary schools in Montreal—in which city the family of the lawyer, now a judge, resided in later years— were all too pleased when he left. This, of course, did not imply that he was unintelligent. He learned only what he liked to learn, and became violently angry when anyone tried to persuade him to tackle other material of instruction. The other schoolmates admired and at the same time feared his boldness in this respect. What he showed was a remarkable preference and ability for drawing and painting, and was passionately fond of gymnastics. It was his love for literature, however, that often kept him up reading the whole night through. We do not know what kind of books he read, but one thing is sure: romanticism made a deep impression on his sensitive being. It shaped the influences which dominated him throughout his lifetime: his love for France and for its heroic past, his admiration for the Middle Ages, all this seen in the mirror of his reading, and his fervent desire to live in Paris, the city from which came most of his spiritual nourishment. In a family less blessed with worldly goods, the conflict between his inclinations and the hard necessities of life might have rapidly taken the boy on the road to disaster; so it was, the family seemed to be happy that Charles felt a strong inclination for at least one kind of activity: his painting. It did not much matter that this kind of profession failed to produce in the majority of cases any income at all.

An American painter, George De Forest-Brush, who visited Pierreville in 1888, not only gave the young man useful painting lessons, but seems to have exercised an influence on him which lasted well beyond their parting. Charles took his painting instruction very seriously, and faithfully visited the School of Painting, an annex of the Art Gallery in Montreal. Eventually, however, he tired of the routine existence and, hardly eighteen years old, he decided to visit for a time, Paris. His teacher and friend De Forest helped to persuade his father to let him go, and recommended him to the painter Gérôme in Paris. Charles' study of painting there was not marked by an excessive zeal; moreover, there was nothing to press him: he knew that every month he would receive ample funds from home. Entirely in keeping with his character he had never given money matters any serious thought, and he knew nothing of the situation of other students who had been less careful in selecting their parents. In the full robustness of his youth and in his nebulous romantic conception he had of real life, he dived immediately into the kind of existence which, in Paris of that period, was referred to as an 'artistic life'. Possibly he persuaded himself that he was blessed with the abilities of a genius and was not merely a painter or a poet. At first he had quarters with respectable people in Batignolles, but he felt that his real life was only with painters and sculptors in their studios. Furthermore he felt at home in the editing rooms of newspapers and above all in the cafés of Montparnasse and Montmartre, the meeting places of new literary talent of that time. Paris of those days with its already slightly decadent bohemianism and the coming 'end-of-the-century' atmosphere, entirely fulfilled his confused expectations. On the other side he was particularly impressed by the beautiful architecture of the French capital, and above all the fine buildings, the numerous mediaeval churches especially the Cathedral of Notre-Dame. Everything here was new for him and in this new world he felt himself as if he had arrived from the moon. He was certainly no exception in thinking that no greater contrast was possible than that existing between the more or less ugly rigidity of the Victorian style combined with the cold industrial and commercial characteristics of Montreal in comparison with the elegance and the easy life of Paris. To him life seemed so congenial in the cafés habituated by new authors, where between the consum of two bocks or vermouths about the whole universum was reformed, or simply changed, where works to accomplish a revolution in literature or art were planned but never executed, where all the burning problems of mankind were entirely solved on a round table by the enthusiastic sons of the Muses wrapped in the hazy atmosphere produced by cigarette smoke, alcoholic fumes and the stale smells of crowded not too often washed bodies. To our young Canadian this was finally the real world he dreamed and records prove that he felt extremely happy in these surroundings. Moreover, he had introductions which opened the doors of many houses; he made the acquaintance of Paul Verlaine and Leconte de Lisle. Gill for several reasons exercised a certain attraction; he came from a country which seemed very far away and was in that period as well as in our time well liked by so many Parisians.

Moreover he was of tall and slender stature and his French fellow-bohemians were already more or less envious of his impressive male profile. His fellows liked him because he loved debating and his clear, melodious voice was attracting many, male and female, to him. One of his contemporaries observed that the sound of his voice seemed to express traces of the harmonious cadences heard rushing in the endless Canadian woods.

So it was that he returned to Montreal in 1892 with a heavy heart. Although he had not studied in Paris with great zeal, it was yet evident that his talent as a painter had developed considerably, and that now he knew how to use correctly and artistically his brush and pen and this with much greater ability than before. He was now twenty-two years old; the age at which most young people of Montreal were already earning sufficient money to cover their cost of living. Desirous of following suit, he opened a studio of his own. Right at the start he had the good fortune to be commissioned by the parson of Notre-Dame church to execute a picture for one of the altars. In addition to this, the order included a study trip to his beloved Paris for a considerable space of time. It is easy to imagine what his feelings were when, after a sojourn of only three months in Canada, he again returned to France. This stay in Paris, which lasted until 1894, changed the artist in many respects; as a man he had become much more mature by the time that he returned to his home country. Again, however, the mentioned unchangeable part of his nature remained very much in evidence. Having finally definitely returned to Montreal, he took the decision to be a professional painter henceforth. Although his talent did not amount to genius it was proved quite genuine, and it had led him to choose this road a few years before with real joy. He painted with much pleasure but did not produce a great number of pictures, nor did he work with great regularity; in addition, now that it was to be the source of his income, he put up a certain resistance to painting. It was the same attitude that he had demonstrated during his school years when someone tried to persuade him to learn a special thing he did not agree. He felt himself subject to strong leanings towards poetry now, which he had always favoured and which he came to value much higher than painting.

A close study of the trends in artistic circles of the Montreal of that period will show that Gill was at the core of a revolutionary movement of young artists. It was the inner revolution against the 'peddler mentality' which nearby everywhere precedes the spiritual upheaval of the young; the production of poetry was not to be associated with the cash sale of artistic products. For romantic artists nothing seems more decadent and abominable than the obligation to use brush, chisel, or lyre for mammon's sake. Symptomatic of these tendencies, the Literary School—École litteraire—was initiated in Montreal. The name is misleading; this was no school, it was a society of artists and poets who met around a table to discuss their own creations together. One of the earliest members was Charles Gill, and certainly he was far from one of the laziest. His zeal, seen from the heights of Pegasus, deserved much praise; but from a materialistic viewpoint it avowedly provided no income whatsoever, and had the extra disadvantage that it left him with very little time for the painting which could and did produce income. But once again providence took good care of him: he received an appointment as professor of drawing at the Jacques Cartier Normal School—École normale. The position provided him with a secure income and at the same time ironically pulled the Bohemian dreamer down to earth and neatly tied him to a very normal run-of-the-mill existence. It is remarkable that he should have held his post over a period of twenty-two years, until shortly before his death. Freed now from the obligation to paint for a living he actually increased his activity, and exhibited several pictures at the annual shows. Later on he broke this habit, not because his inclination for painting had diminished, but because he believed that the panel of judges failed to show the right measure of appreciation for his works. It should be mentioned that during these years Gill had a strong leaning

towards the study of astronomy and physics. Being certain of
his livelihood, he neither took these studies too seriously, nor
did he feel inclined to paint, except for his own pleasure.
Amongst the harvest we find many excellent portraits, landscapes, portrayals of Montreal, particularly from the slopes of
Mount Royal, and several pictures to fix his memories of Sorel.
Some of the landscapes, especially those produced during his
last years of activity, are very fine and honour his artistic
talent. Others again, such as 'The Inspiration', show a weak
romanticism of a second-hand nature.

But it would be too easy to dismiss Gill quickly as a mediocre
artist who produced a fair number of pictures. This kind of
criticism must give way on contemplating his picture 'The
Chess Problem', which has the typical featherlight brush
technique of a great artist and belongs to the class of international importance. The lovable old greybeard, meditating
his next move on the chessboard before him, seems to reflect
all the experience of a long and studious life in his nearly
transparent countenance. With thoughtful caution he seems to
ponder the consequences of the next move on the chessboard
of life. The picture has been endlessly reproduced, and colour-
prints of it are to be found in almost every country throughout
the world. For a just appreciation of Gill's work as a painter
one must give 'The Chess Problem' detailed attention. It has
already been shown that Gill was not a painter in the true
sense of the word. He felt that he had general artistic gifts, a
consistent artistic nature somewhat similar to that conjectured
by romanticists as belonging to the genius of a Leonardo da
Vinci. He did not, therefore, at all mind disregarding specific
forms of artistic expression if he felt that he could better
interpret the worlds of light and colour, of spirit and feeling,
with other means at his disposal. At one time he evidenced
particular favour for musical expression and played the violin,
just as he found in chess—which he played extremely well—
yet another expression of the problems and tensions of life.
The most important period of artistic development for Charles
Gill seems to have been the years between 1895 and 1909.

He appears to have clearly realised that a particular period of his life had come to an end on his returning to Canada in 1895; the time of his youth and the gay days of the student were closed for this young man of twenty-five. His years in France have provided him with many valuable experiences, but to some extent they remained without value as he was unable to see that they were, after all, events in a strange world that could not provide the intimate contacts for his spirit, only given by the emanations of the country of his birth. But life in his own country represented a direct contact with everyday reality, and many unpleasant questions with regard to his own future, long pushed aside, now demanded his full attention.

All this would not have been very important for the average type of young man who straight from playful school-life adjusts to his father's social position and becomes his junior business partner. Gill, however, was anything but a normal son. He was a combination of an athlete of old Hellas with superb strength and bodily development, and a most modern and slightly decadent romantic with an excess of sensitiveness. Companionship and pity were exalted to a high degree. In his conception, the romantic artist and the Parisian bohemian represented the only type of a true man. The only values in life were the beauties of poetry as produced by Lamartine, Hugo, Goethe and Verlaine, and the pictures painted by the greatest past and present artists of Europe. No doubt an aesthetic philosophy of life which had only the defect to be one sided. So Gill enjoyed his happiest moments when reciting poetry, and at such times he often wept tears of emotion. It is easy to understand that, given this idea of the 'good-life', he did not much care about the requirements of material existence. This lack of concern to give proper thought to the needs of everyday existence in a material world is strongly expressed in some of his verse forming the first part of an ambitious national poem dedicated to the city of Montreal. These verses are not particularly flattering to the inhabitants of Montreal, nor to Montreal itself, any more than are those of Samuel

Butler: he expresses a deep revulsion and even hatred towards this Canadian 'Babylon', as he calls it. One may find exaggeration in the straining of the contrasts, but at the same time one thing should be realised: this young man who entered in this city the domain of material things was the bearer of a spiritual torch. Openly, and for the benefit of all his countrymen, he carried the light of a culture liberated from secondary interests into an Elysian field. There was no other historical or political author or poet in the country able to match him in this respect.

From their beginning the young professor of drawing was a regular visitor to the literary gatherings in the Château Ramezay, meeting place of the promising group of such well-known authors, poets and painters as Frechette, Ferland, Charbonneau, Nelligan, and Lozeau. During this period Gill wrote for newspapers; his style was fluid and expressive. From 1896 on he published in these papers some of his poems, which later were edited under the title 'Shooting Stars'. He married in 1902, but his marriage remained without essential influence on his personality and artistic ability. Gradually, Gill let his brush rest and preferred his pen for the portrayal of the things he wanted to convey to his countrymen and to the world at large. Inwardly, this change was completed when, on the 24th of February in 1909, he took a sheet of paper and wrote the title of an epic poem which had been in his thoughts for a long time: 'Le Saint Laurent—The St. Lawrence'.

It might be useful to mention here that throughout his life Gill was victim of a kind of self-deception—perhaps quite voluntary—with regard to his own personality; he liked to see himself as a bohemian and vagabond. But to what extent was he that which he believed himself? The years of his boyhood prove nothing in particular; if physicians had been asked, they might possibly have said something about glandular disorder and the crises of puberty. Life as Gill could observe it in his family circle and amongst his teachers flowed easily and without upheaval. His father was a well-balanced 'dyed in grain' conservative. It may be possible that through young Charles'

veins ran some of the blood of his energetic grandfather
Senécal. Apart from this there was nothing that could have
induced him to particular zeal of activity; money necessity
least of all. Already as a boy he had tried to neutralise his
excessive sensitivity by adventurous and even dangerous
sports; the result was that he had developed his body to that
of a gladiator, but nevertheless his soul had remained as
sensitive as before. Literary romanticism provided him with
sufficient justification to take his rebel stand against a world—
in his opinion—seemingly destitute of any deep sentiment. But
his road by the way of Lamartine did not lead him to the
English or German kind of romanticism; rather to the French
variety which embodied also a strong national feeling together
with an unscattered Christian faith. This was in France a
general reaction against the atheistic philosophy inherited
from the eighteenth century of 'enlightenment'. It was not the
education received from his family and at school which shaped
his personality; it was the fusion of his predisposition for
romanticism and the actual experience of it abroad. He saw
Paris, France, Sorel and Montreal through the glasses of a
romantic; but these glasses were fashioned in such a way that
everything he did not see in Paris was observed with particular
clarity in his home country, especially in the 'Babylon' named
Montreal, with another word, all things in Paris were white
and those of Montreal only black. This has to be mentioned
in order to a better understanding of our poet and expressing
that is not at all an attempt to suggest that culture and way of
life towards the end of the nineteenth century were similar in
Montreal and in Paris.

The number of the Parisian artist-bohemians had considerably increased in the mentioned period and their way of life,
very different from that poetically embroidered by Giacomo
Puccini in his opera, had developed in the confused heads
into something similar to a religious faith or at least justified
as to be a historical necessity. Adherents of this way of disorderly way of life, of laziness, of alcoholism and debauch
were moreover convinced that they were the only true heirs of

romanticism. Here it would be useful to remember the fate of poets who went this way, for example Heine, Musset and Charles Baudelaire. Gill did not find it necessary to deny that these aforesaid pretensions were not altogether justified. It should also be mentioned that the Parisian bohemian was a cosmopolitan being and Christianism as well as Christian morals meant little to him and he often seemed to reflect a confused reminder of the pantheism or atheism of the century of the 'enlightenment'. Seen in retrospect this bohemian thinking remind some modern kinds of nihilistic existentialism at present en vogue in France. Nevertheless it is true that genuine Romanticism fought a real and in its tendencies understandable battle against void and empty formalism. But soon the movement deteriorated in a battle against windmills, like that of Don Quixote, and fell into an abandonment of all respect for the old immanent code of moral cleanliness, aesthetics and ethics. Evidently, even in bohemian circles themselves, there was a considerable difference between the bohemian 'salons' which in a certain sense were conservative and only specialised in unusual attire of the visitors; the proletarian kind of bohemians, who added the grease spots and broken buttons to their coats, and finally the numerous studios, most of them filthy with layers of dirt and absinth-drinking decadents, syphilitics moving in their moral and spiritual darkness.

It was fortunate for Gill that he did not venture beyond the limits of the aforesaid 'salons' and the more or less bourgeois-clean studios. On this side of the limits the accent was rather on a pleasant, artistic way of life, the eloquent gestures of coffee-shop authors and of misunderstood painters with ambitious plans which, of course, were never realised. Gill's nature was uncritical and he did not know what hard and purposeful work really meant. It is not difficult to understand that he felt entirely at home in his special bohemian world and saw himself as a link between his present and the romanticism of Lamartine, the latter considered as an ally and as a justification for his battle against that what he called the brutal and detestable materialism of Montreal. In this respect his picture 'The Chess Problem' seems to be a psychologically expressed hint that he was fully aware of the materialistic antagonists in this city and, being cautious, did not intend to make a fresh move until acquainted with him adversaries' intentions.

He actually finished a fragment of his epic, showing in each word a flaming protest against all sorts of materialism, namely love of money, and lack of culture or civilised manners. With sovereign indifference he disregards everything that represents the material richness of his country, and he uses his epic to stress, for his own and for future generations, whatever stands in Canadian life for culture and for eternal, indestructible values. Charles Gill intended that his country—that is especially the St. Lawrence River district—should be the heir and preserver to his epic, which in length, volume and bold-ness was meant to match like qualities of the magnificent river. He projected a poem of ten volumes, of which—rather typically—only the last volume was actually produced. It bears the title 'Cape Eternity'. The volume contains a pro-logue and twelve hymns, although they do not all appear to have been written originally for this purpose. Apart from the hymns, the 'Song to the Stars' and the patriotic confession 'Fatherland' finish the book. The prologue relates the fiction of Gill's visit to the Bay of St. John on the Saguenay River where he had to remain for several days while awaiting a favourable wind which would permit his sailing boat to con-tinue the voyage. The boredom of the delay induces him to ask the hospitable fisherman's family where he is staying for something to read. At first the fisherman replies that there is nothing, but he remembers later that a long time previously a traveller had left a notebook behind full of writing. Gill reads the notebook and learns that a young man—Gill's double in the poem—has fled from babylonic Montreal to this point. Happy to be freed of the crass materialism of the big city, this comparatively isolated spot revives his memory of the proud, intrepid Indian race which had once lived in the surrounding mountains. They had adopted the Christian faith at an early date and were true friends of the French-Canadian settlers.

The youth had attempted to cross the river in a small Indian craft made of bark, and approaching night and the impending storm obliged him to find shelter in Tadoussac:

'The last light of day was on the point of fading,
For a long, weary time I had been expecting to reach the
    shore,
The formidable north bank of wild, steep cliffs,
Where the black Saguenay, River of Death,
Gushes forth from a cleft torn in the flank of the rocks
To thrust into the St. Lawrence its full sweep of waters.
As night came on the shoreline seemed to loom larger,
And even more appalling became the darkness with woe-
    ful sound,
The moaning of waters that rose in confused mutterings
    and sighing.
The placid swell about me had grown to giant waves,
A mass of dense grey clouds obscured the sky;
The seabirds hastened to their lofty shelters:
Even the gulls, swiftly mounting higher and higher,
Among the frightful cliffs sought their refuge.
Frantically playing my oars I struggled to land,
But, exhausted in vain, I approached no nearer.
Transfused to a sombre brown were the purple moun-
    tains,
Vainly had I hoped to cross before nightfall,
Since in the dark the fearful summits
Mislead calculation and deceive the sight.
Now, upon the calamitous heaving of the waves,
Night fall, a night of horror, without starlight, awful,
Falling on me, victim of fate, like a bird of prey.
I struggled to stifle in the billows' din
The voice of memory weeping in my soul;
Vainly I fled from the sorrows of other days,
From the bitter remorse welling up in my heart.'

Landing at Tadoussac at long last, he ascends to the little

church of which the bell suddenly starts to ring of its own accord. The sound revives his memories of the proud and courageous Indians who had once inhabited these mountains. Bitterly he compares their heroic conduct with the present citizens of Montreal. He loses himself in thought, and has a vision of the last famous tribal chief, Tacouerima. Gill, or his double, addresses him as one of the living dead, a tragic fugitive from the present of which he despairs. Tacouerima, however, points out the youth's mission to him, saying:

> 'Be famous through your grief and sing the glory of the country.'

In order to attain this stage of poetic purification he now decides to navigate the black stream. Tacouerima provides him with two assistants to help him finish his work: Silence and Forgetfulness:

> 'Silence plied his velvet pinions, and preceding Forgetfulness,
> As always, he took his place in the bows of my boat,
> Forgetfulness, however, sat by me in the stern, and placed his cheek my icy brow;
> Then the angel pressed his eternal lips on my brow,
> Scored with many lines of grief, and enveloped me in the shadow of his wings.
> His spirit interfused with mine, and in the celestical shudder of that divine kiss,
> Infinite peace settled at last in my bosom.
> From memory the angel hid me with his wide wing.
> All vanished away: affliction, bitterness, remorse.
> Heavenly forgiveness flooded through my heart,
> And through my immortal soul swept the breath of God.'

He travels the Saguenay against the stream, symbol of his struggle against materialism. The portrayal of the heroic landscape of the river as it flows between terror-inspiring mountain cliffs—the adversaries—is one of the most beautiful parts of the epic. Impressed by the majesty of Nature the lonely navigator sings:

> 'O my poor country, mayst thou, by thy mighty streams,
> For thy gross multitude of petty men, be forgiven!'

With the first light of the new day he arrives at Eternity Bay. The two angels who kept him company now disappear together with the mist of the night, and enveloped in the early light of the dawning day he exclaims:

> 'Teach me how with serene countenance to scale
> The holy summits which lead to the stars.'

This appeal he certainly did not address to any of his countrymen or even to the genii of the place. He addressed it to Alighieri Dante, who was for him, and also presently for a great number of historians, the exponent of a vast Christian universal culture not yet spoiled by decadence or the following Renaissance. He appeals to Dante to be told the secret of how he and his Canadian people can scale the heights to where mankind's face can touch the spirit of the stars. The second part of his request seems to contain the response of the greatest poet of the end of the Middle-Ages:

> 'O Bay of Eternity, how I love thy dark waves!
> Thy fathomless bed cuts through the stark rock
> Convulsively rising into sheer peaks,
> Preserving forever the tragic imprint of Chaos.
> To the wild verge of this abysmal river
> Henceforward art compels me to sing.
> But alas! I struggle in vain to utter
> Its power divine, at once sublime and fearful.'

It continues in the same dantesque strain, and in the next canto 'Ave Maria', he obtains a response to his last doubt. He sees from Cape Eternity, on the lower platform of the mighty structure of Cape Trinity, the statue of the Queen of Heaven. This vision he interprets as a divine sign, and now knows that only faith and love are able to provide the true and correct inspiration for his art. His poem reaches dramatic heights in

the ninth canto 'Cape Eternity'. The poet in this vision desires
to understand the significance and fate of these enormous
silent witnesses, these masses of mountains, throughout the
centuries. Mankind seems insignificant confronted with such
supreme creations of God's power and splendour:

> 'They have seen the consummation of fearful destinies,
> But nothing has altered their fearful aspect.
> They have seen all things change about them,
> Yet have avoided the law of all earthly things.
> Yes, all things have they seen alter about them,
> All things born, all things die in their turn,
> All reborn, live a little time, and wither into death,
> Great pines and ropes of ivy flourished on their flanks,
> And perished in the whirlwind of ages with the genera-
>   tions of man,
> His tears and his laughter, weaknesses and strength,
> His towns and his cities, little known realms and mighty
>   Empires!'

The tenth canto, 'Dream and Intelligence', explains somewhat academically by way of comparison with both capes, the
insight the poet has gained regarding God's ruling of the
world. This canto is in blank verse, as distinguished from the
Alexandrines of the others. The eleventh canto 'To the Top',
is a new and powerful impulse towards a confession of the
beauty of Nature and of the manifest sublimity and love of
God:

> 'Now I enter the community of this vast love
> Which rises from the earth to the embracing sun.'

The last canto 'The Ant', is the epilogue, and it once more
makes all the beauty of creation glow. Man himself stands in
the centre of this imposing picture, but he realises his triviality
and therefore recognises the limitations of human intellect and
human activity; he is resigned, but at the same time he is free
and happy. The verses addressed to the stars, actually an
expression of Gill's conception of the meaning of life, and

likewise the short patriotic verses 'Fatherland', if at all supposed to form part of the poem, might have perhaps better served as an introduction, before the Prologue. The completed section, planned as the torso only of a more majestic and impressive poem, presents itself as a drama of human soul fighting a battle for the orientation of its own personality and for the spiritual expression of a people or a nation. Clearly, this is not an epic closing a cultural period, like the heroic poems of the Middle Ages. Canada is still young as a nation, and the soil of this enormous country is as yet virgin for the better part. Traditions are beginning to take shape, and an independent culture is commencing to reshape the inheritance of the population. Gill's epic can be likened to the Minoan foundations which even old Hellas required for the construction of its own proud home.

A modest man, and accustomed to self criticism, Gill had prophetic moments in conceiving himself as one of the designers of this beginning. We may add: not one of the least, although it has as yet not been fully recognised. Many historic figures have gradually disappeared into the darkness of time, and it is remarkable that the apparition of this poet, instead of disappearing, exacts recognition.

During his later years Gill suffered much through paralytic trouble that curtailed his literary production. After a short illness he died on the 16th of October 1918.

James Wilson Morrice

The so-called 'topographers' and 'regionalists' were the first artists in the field of Canadian painting. They were the painters who, like Paul Kane or Cornelius Krieghoff, endeavoured to portray the local landscape with its people and its work as faithfully as possible: just as they saw it with their own eyes. Since any man can only see himself and his world through the glasses and in the perspective of his own time, there is no reason to reproach painters for such a characteristic.

Canada did not have a technique of painting all its own, and so it was imported from Europe. The Canadian feature in the artists' work was, first of all, the range of objects which served for portrayal. The work was Canadian in so far the artist succeeded in catching in his picture the specific 'fluidity' of the Canadian scene and of the persons he painted. The painter Kane, who often painted Indians with the stature of ancient Roman citizens and whose prairie horses look like Arabian thoroughbreds, was less successful than Krieghoff in portraying this particular element. The 'Topographers' clearly painted with the technique of the old Dutch painting school, which understood the art of introducing psychology, without any ostentation into the total impression of a picture. They did not care, therefore, to produce pictures of which the significance and quality had to be explained to the laymen by art-experts. Their portrayal of a human body or a landscape was the same as conceived by the majority of mankind.

This view, which lasted throughout the earlier history of West-European painting, gradually lost favour towards the end of the nineteenth century. The tendency originated in the

Parisian ateliers and gradually made itself felt in all countries, including Canada. It is the period of a number rather mixed and confused modern movements, which maintain that the means of expression used by painters so far are antiquated and exhausted. This is, at least, one aspect of the situation. It cannot be denied, however, that at the same time opponents of the new movements maintained that force of expression and eagerness for difficult and exhausting labour, are no more to be found amongst modern painters. Even when one takes a neutral stand, the result of a careful comparison—without trying to find the basic causes—must be that the former painstaking art of drawing and the penetrating treatment of detail seem to be superfluous for modern painters. In a subsequent period of this development even the subject of the painting becomes unimportant, and something intangible, generally labelled as 'mood' or 'atmosphere', is given the highest preference.

The adherents of this new art, however, when they find the expression of this mood or atmosphere in works of their predecessor—eventually the Romanticists—decry it as 'sentimental junk' without even investigating the means by which such a 'mood' has been produced. Perhaps not entirely without importance is the opinion of the public, the layman, to whom in last analysis every painting is addressed. To him, this modern fashion, which is in constant revolution, appears as a very strange palette constantly growing in muddiness. It is undeniable that appreciation of art, as practised by cultured people of our times, has not come to them just by chance or out of the clouds; the appreciation of art in Western Europe has developed continuously from the aesthetic and ethical conceptions of Humanism. It is not difficult to see that the art-loving public still adheres to these expressions and forms, created on the basis of humanistic ideals, even in our own period, during which they have been abandoned by the painters themselves. Therefore, if there is any question with regard to the alienation between public and painter, the fault is largely on the side of the Painter.

Occasionally, the public has not failed to make its opinions known, as is born out by anecdotes such as the visit of the Archduke Franz Ferdinand of Austria to a Kokoschka exhibition, or the same opinion of the statesman and painter Churchill regarding modern painting. It does not appear, however, that these many warnings and admonitions have been heeded. Nowadays there exists a mood of battle between the painters and the public, in which the latter is at a disadvantage, as the majority of contemporary painters has already joined easy, revolutionary 'modernism'. Even the museums of today are often crammed with their works. Nevertheless, modern painters cannot obtain the much desired victory in this battle, because they antagonise even the serious reformers amongst the public by an increased production of nonsensical painting which tries to find expression in geometrical absurdities and wild application of colour, and often shows pathological aspects.

The first wave of modernism in art reaching the Canadian shore, was instrumental in leading to the formation of groups of painters such as the 'Group of Seven' in Toronto. They attempted to reconcile opposite values which actually cannot be reconciled. These efforts had, in the beginning, a new nationalistic flavour. In some way or other, and notwithstanding the enthusiasm for the new technique of painting imported from Paris, there was a vague awareness of the decadent qualities apparent in European painting, or—and this is essentially the same thing—it was believed that this young nation, which had not as yet developed painting as an art of its own, would well be able to produce the same art as Europe has produced in centuries. The slogan for these groups was therefore the cry: 'Free from Europe'. This is, seen in itself, an excellent word, but it had the single defect that for the purpose of effecting the separation, only the painting techniques imported from Europe itself were available.

The attempt made to overcome this weak point was by looking exclusively in the Canadian landscape for the subjects of painting; this was in itself, not at all a new departure. It was hoped that, by this method, the resistance of the Canadian public against the new fashion of painting (which resistance was called 'academic') could be vanquished fairly easily. If this aim has been attained in the past, it cannot be affirmed with a full measure of assurance today. Part of the success achieved is due to the erroneous opinion that an independent and pure Canadian art had made its appearance. Several painters such as Maurice Cullen (1866–1934) and Aurele Suzor-Coté (1869–1937), men of excellent talent, actively contributed to giving shape to this opinion, although—out of caution perhaps—they used only the best elements of the new school of painting, such as the wider range of colours and the treatment of light, when producing their own works. The best method, however, of studying this period of revolutionary art and the search for a new orientation in Canadian painting, is by concentrating on a single young man whose spirit seemed to represent the full essence of this new world, with all its artistic and mental problems: one James Wilson Morrice.

He was born on the 10th of August, 1865, in Montreal; his parents originally came from the central part of Scotland. Certain national characteristics of the Scottish people seem to have crystallised to an unusual degree in his family. In their life there was no place for the sunny carefree joviality, which is so common in France and in Central Europe. Just like the sky of Scotland—rarely sunny and blue—and like the sea on her shores, everything seemed extremely serious and all sentiment remained hidden in the depths of the soul, banished by immovable conventions. Here were people with an iron tranquillity and with an extremely distrustful reserve as far as the outer world was concerned. The parents were wealthy and were well received by the highest levels of Montreal society; they lived simply, however, and in a discreet way gave support to many charities and artistic movements in the city. This, and the family collection of beautiful paintings, are our only clues to the existence of an artistic vein in the circle.

After finishing High School, James went to Toronto to study law. It often happens to children of well-to-do families that they have no inclination for the profession of the business-man; James was no exception. During his years as a student he seems to have remained entirely undecided with regard to his future career. Since High School he had a certain inclina-tion for drawing and painting; he had also believed himself to have a certain talent for both. Perhaps this was not as much a conscious orientation as a revolt against the study of law, which seemed extremely long and tedious; in any case, paint-ing had already become his hobby during his days as a student. A few of his pictures painted in this period have been pre-served; they are not particularly perfect, nor remarkable for any other reason. They represent the correct work of a pupil in the traditional style of watercolour. If there is any departure from tradition at all, it might be found in the fact that—as against the crowded paintings of that period—his works looked somewhat empty, which perhaps can be explained by his Scottish nature. Nor is it surprising for a Scotsman, that the serious industry which he dedicated to this hobby, was at a par with his real or intended career. Certainly great labour was necessary to develop the talent which showed only small indications of existence.

Apparently our student was reading a great deal on the subjects of painting and the life of painters in Paris. After finishing his study at the University without any measure of enthusiasm—but with fair success—he was definitely faced with the choice of a career, and decided quite simply to be-come a painter. In order to learn all the fundamentals of this art, he decided to continue his studies in Paris, the Mecca of painting and bohemian life. After some deliberation, his parents consented, and James left for France, well provided with money and good intentions.

James Wilson Morrice, a level-headed and uncommuni-cative young man, was not one to abandon himself to the heady champagne of Parisian life, with its artists and authors, all in an 'end-of-the-century' mood. It rather seems as if this frivolous life spurred him to a greater measure of reserve, to the extent that he moved less in these circles than he did in the

English artistic centres of the French capital. It seemed to appeal to him more since here, confidences were neither given nor expected in return: the former he would have found most uninteresting, the latter, impossible. Taking stock of all that we know of Morrice, he had not—as could perhaps be assumed —an egotistic nature in the active sense of the word. He could have been termed egocentric, and it is well known that this kind of person likes to establish solid relations with the outer world, and that beyond these, nothing has any interest for him. These well-established relations are the single track by which happenings in the outerworld are allowed to approach, so that they can be stopped well in advance, in case they threatened to disturb the balance of mind. Keeping this well in mind, it is not difficult to explain the fact that Morrice frequently met authors and painters like Somerset Maugham or Matisse; these artists only rarely mention Morrice, and if they do the information is rather vague. Where temperaments of a different order found warm friendships or strong hostility, Morrice was quite satisfied to have neutral relationships which tended to prevent self-expression. It is easy to understand therefore, that all these people who were kept at a distance took little note of his personality, and concentrated their full interest on his works. In this unusual way Morrice obtained what he had been longing for all his life.

He was of normal stature, if not slightly smaller; a somewhat broad head and long face rested on a strong neck; his forehead was high, an impression enhanced by the fact that he grew bald early. His eyes were brilliant and somewhat prominent, perhaps already indicating latent thyroid gland disorder and its accompanying emotional upheavals; his mouth seemed rather sensual, with heavy pronounced lips. A short beard framed his face, and the total impression was less that of a painter than of a physician or a professor. He was entirely lacking the appearance popularly attributed to followers of the Muses. He approached his art in a positive, matter-of-fact way, just as a factory hand starts his job, or an artisan his task.

He avoided all appearances common to the amateur; any place where he lived and worked revealed a cool professional attitude. He even limited his mental interests to those spheres directly related with painting. If we succeed at all in combining these elements for shaping a mental profile of the artist, we must arrive at the conclusion that Morrice, even if he had developed a superb technique, could never have been the equal of a Jean-Auguste-Dominique Ingres or a William Turner. His sober somewhat empty nature, did not allow him to produce artistic work of the cultural depth and breadth of European painting; on the other hand, it saved him from participating in the madness of the 'Independents'. And finally, it predestined him to seek a road of simplification and extreme sobriety of human sentiment in painting, and as such he became Canada's most talented artist in this particular field.

It would be a regrettable error to assume that our limiting evaluation of Morrice's personality could be interpreted as a depreciation of the man and artist. The opposite is true. To destroy the false notions of assumed character traits which fantasy has woven around him, will help us to see his personality and his work in a clear, true, and objective light. Only thus is it possible to appreciate his real qualities. Morrice was a lonely man, a man, who silently went through life, without histrionic qualities, not involved in scandals, not wishing for any publicity or public appreciation. His road was dictated from within, by his own peculiar character, and whatever the world might have said of what he did and how he did it, left him unmoved. Even if he were not an artist, such a character would be remarkable in human society. Being an artist, it is indeed highly interesting and unusual that he was able to keep his ideals unblemished notwithstanding his confessed sympathy with the modern technique of painting; notwithstanding also the high waves of controversy in art which moved Paris at that time.

He lived in that city in unpretentious residences; small homes without luxury or in upper stories of old tenement houses on the shores of the Seine; first on the Quai des Grands Augustins; last somewhat higher upstream on the Quai de la Tournelle. These homes leave the visitor with the sole impression of a professional workshop. They contained only the most essential pieces of furniture, and the better part of the artist's belongings could be found in well-packed trunks, as if the owner had always to be prepared to leave at any moment. All this certainly was an exception to the common type of 'ateliers' to be found in Paris. It was neither mundane nor slovenly; the owner was neither a Bohemian in the Parisian sense nor an ascetic. Morrice had the habit of dressing elegantly, using the best English materials; he liked good meals and had no aversion towards spirits in all drinkable shapes and forms. Regarding the latter, he liked them so much that he needed their uplift, particularly during his later years, in order to practise his art. He did not like women particularly and this might have been the reason why he never married.

Not all his visitors may have noticed—and, if they did, they may not have given the fact much attention—that from his window he had a wide perspective of the River Seine, with the never-ceasing movement of ships and lighters and the ever-changing life on the quays, immersed during summer in the leaves of the trees. A painter could not have asked for a better incentive. The French State, and later the National Gallery in Ottawa, obtained his pictures 'The Quai des Grands Augustins', belonging to the best work he produced outside Canada. These pictures, produced around the year 1902, show, with typical waywardness, his individual technique of painting notwithstanding all the influences of the modern schools which surrounded him. There is no evasive, uncertain play of light over his pictures; his light is static, flat and attached to objects. All colours, even those of a clear daylight scene, show some relation with grey, just as if a slightly colour-blind person had produced them. It is thought that Morrice accepted this fashion from Whistler, for whom he had a great esteem. Perhaps it would be more correct to say that his individual colour scheme was in line with his own nature, and that unconsciously and regardless of his own will he expressed in this way the inner sadness of his soul. All his paintings have this same feature, and they therefore show a peculiar gloominess. Even the vivid colours which he was forced to reproduce in the West Indies, are unable to fully overcome this disposition as expressed in his painting.

When Morrice left Canada for the first time, with the purpose of taking up residence in Paris, it looked as if it would produce a definite separation from his home country, which seemed to have lost all significance for him or to have become slightly repellent. However, he did not have the ability to become acclimatised in France. Apart from the fact that throughout his life his knowledge of the French language remained rudimentary, he obviously always took his mysterious Nordic personality with him. Even his best acquaintances referred to him only as 'The Canadian'. His loneliness, made more acute through his separation from his family, seems to have contributed to improve his contact with Canada; whatever the main reason, he visited his own country regularly until 1914 and always sent his pictures to the exhibitions in Canadian cities.

In 1896 he started on a voyage to Italy and North Africa, chiefly with the aim of sojourning there during a good part of the winter. It is remarkable that for his sojourns in Canada he nearly always chose the winter season. Here he painted the twenty-six pictures of which we have knowledge and which have a Canadian subject. A work representative of his art, produced in Canada, 'Ferry from Quebec' is now owned by the National Gallery in Ottawa. The shores of the St. Lawrence River are deeply covered by snow, and the steamer, seeming somewhat over-large in the picture, navigates through seagreen waters and ice-floes towards the shore of the opposite situated Levis. The high talent of Morrice is well represented in this excellent picture, as well as in his winter landscape 'Mountainslope near Quebec', an impressive picture of the sternness and wildness of winter in this country. People who have never visited Canada in that season, will get a fair impression of what winter means in this country, by giving this picture their full attention. It will be clear that before all it is the mood of winter which we experience in these pictures.

What else is really Canadian in these paintings is hard to say, notwithstanding the clear geographical indications contained in their names. Their topography alone is too general and too vague to actually recognise the locality, excepted the picture from Quebec city. The brushwork is hard and purposely limited to mere indications. Perspectives are observed only to some extent; people and horses are painted in natural attitudes, but in a shadowy way. As a whole these portrayals are excellent examples of the recent mutation in the art of painting: from Form to lack of Form. Just because Morrice stands at the crossroads of this transition, and because, through the monotony of his paintings, we still get the merest glimpse of a recollection of youth and an inclination towards a different way of painting, his work is of intense interest to us.

This might explain why adherents of the modern tendencies in painting will exclaim 'excellent!' when looking at his pictures. Conservatives, however, might walk off with a quiet feeling of pity. Pity, because Morrice does not belong to those wizards of the canvas, who first get their conception of Nature straightened out, and then produce their so called 'moods' with fairly little trouble. Morrice conveys through his pictures a harmony of Nature and from this quality may derive the opinion that poetry is alive in his heart.

Since his first departure from Canada, Morrice was a restless wanderer; one is tempted to say: a man without roots. He was in Africa during several winters preceding World War I; two of these he spent in Tangier, together with Matisse and Marquet. His pictures of war scenes, produced as a result of orders received for them, do not deserve any special attention, not even in his own opinion. As a result of the death of his parents, his contacts with Canada diminished. He often travelled to the West Indies. When asked by a friend why he made these trips, he dismissed the question with the reply, 'A painter must travel southwards; it cleans his palette'. It cannot be said of him that his art was perfected in the last years of his life, although the true followers of modern art classify one of his last paintings, 'The Bay of Trinity', as his real masterpiece. Apart from the two figures of people bathing in the Bay, which are painted in a well-defined manner, the whole design of the painting makes a confused impression. The man who painted this picture was already ill; it is a man in bad health, who needs heavy stimulants to keep the painter's brush moving. Returning to France, he intends to sojourn in North Africa during the winter in order to find a cure, or at least an alleviation of his sufferings, even though he does not believe they are fatal. On the road to Africa he passes away in the Tunis hospital on the 23rd of January 1924. Later in the same year his friends in Paris organised a memorial exhibition of his works in the Salon d'Automne, of which he was a member.

His biography appeared in Canada in the year 1937 and the National Gallery in Ottawa arranged a retrospective showing in the same year displaying almost the full range of his works. Nowadays, paintings of James Wilson Morrice can be found in all Canadian Museums; in particular they are numerous in the Fine Arts Gallery in Montreal. Without any doubt they form a prominent and important testimony to the historical development of the art of painting in Canada.

Cornelius Krieghoff

The records of the Catholic church at Düsseldorf in Germany make mention of the fact that Johann Krieghoff was a Master Upholsterer of the city, and in 1806 married the daughter of a merchant from Rotterdam by the name of Wouters. He had four children of which the youngest was Cornelius, born in May 1812. Originally, father Krieghoff seems to have come from Hamburg; the name Krieghoff is met with frequency in the western part of Northern Germany. Johann Krieghoff was a fairly wealthy man who was interested in the arts, particularly in music.

Cornelius seems to have inherited the artistic vein of his father; the parents decided to allow him an education in music and painting. As he had an excellent ear for music, Cornelius found no difficulty in learning to play several instruments: the violin, guitar, flute and piano. When sixteen years old he was sent to relatives in Schwienfurt, where he obtained further instruction in painting as well as a sound general education. After a sojourn of two years, the young man returned to Düsseldorf on receiving the sudden news that his father had passed away unexpectedly.

From this event onwards his life shows a marked difference from the pattern of small-town citizenship which he had followed so far. Together with a friend, who apparently was also an artist, he started to roam the world. The two bohemians travelled as wandering musicians through Germany, Austria, Italy and France onward to his mother's country, Holland. In order to earn his living, every now and then he did some painting. He seems to have remained for about two years in

Rotterdam at the home of his mother's relatives, where he conscientiously studied several arts, particularly painting, and interested himself in botany. It seems, however, that notwithstanding his serious efforts, the young man was unable to find a satisfactory living in the Dutch commercial city; or perhaps he could not settle down in what seemed to him a city of philistines and yielded to the urge to travel in search of adventures. At any rate, early in 1837 he left for New York, probably in order to be able to visit from there his older brother Ernst, a resident of Toronto. The romantically-inclined youth evidently had taken a wrong view of the spirit prevalent in the American metropolis. Arriving without any money, his only opportunity was to join the ranks of the American army, which was looking for volunteers for the battle against the insurrection of the Seminole Indians in Florida.

It was evident from the start that he did not seek military distinction; quite the contrary, he tried to use his own talents. He became attached to the group of artists sponsored by the Army staff for the purpose of producing paintings of military events for the benefit of posterity. Records of the American Secretary of War prove that Cornelius acquitted himself faithfully of his task by producing a hundred pen and crayon drawings. Unfortunately, these drawings have not so far been traced in the archives, possibly through lack of real interest.

The Americans rewarded the value of the artistic services rendered by promoting Cornelius to corporal. After three years' service he was honourably discharged from his regiment at Burlington, in the State of Vermont, on the 5th of May 1840. It is not known what induced him to rejoin the army the same day and at the same time to disappear from Burlington. This unusual behaviour might perhaps have some connection with a love-affair, which had started about a year and a half before, in New York. There he had made the acquaintance of a particularly lovely and intelligent French-Canadian, Louise Gauthier, from Longueuil near Montreal. This young girl worked in New York as a servant. Her parents were settlers, peasants who obtained their livelihood from their farm and occasional cartage job—sufficient to keep them from real financial worry. Apparently it was love at first sight and trustworthy records mention that they were married in 1839 by the Catholic vicar in Manhattan. It is understood that the young couple went straightaway to Toronto, where Cornelius's elder brother operated a photographic or similar workshop. In 1841 a daughter was born and baptised Emilie, after the Christian name of the elder Mrs. Krieghoff. After their sojourn in Toronto during a time which has not been specified, the young couple and their baby daughter travelled to Longueuil where they were received with warm kindness by the parents of Louise. The tall, slender young man with his lively hazel eyes, thick blonde hair and attractive well-coloured features, soon became a favourite of the Gauthier family. This sympathy was particularly due to his possession of something foreign, refined and intellectual, accompanied by easy and pleasant manners, the result of wide and diversified travels.

The Gauthier's could hardly know that this young man was a fair sample of the Bohemian mind produced in increasing quantity in the Holy Roman Reich of the German nation since the Thirty Years War. Many of us will remember similar groups of youth who after the first World War wandered through many countries in their shorts and with a guitar as their only piece of luggage. They were like leaves which the storm of the mankind's history had torn from their own country's trees and blown far away into foreign territory. Many of these young people had fine talents, but often these perished with them before attaining full development. Only a few could save themselves from the storm and settle down. All these human beings were doomed to unusual fates which Nietzsche would without hesitation have classified as being 'beyond good and evil'. Therefore during the whole of their existence their contemporaries either looked upon them with a measure of distaste or with undisguised surprise. Perhaps we can best do justice to Cornelius Krieghoff if we contemplate his life from this particular point of view.

Did Krieghoff feel the call to become a painter? Did he

have an artistic nature the same as for example Turner, Courbet or Böcklin? Most likely no. It is quite possible that Krieghoff never seriously looked upon himself as an artist of certain merit. Young Cornelius possessed an excellent if not perfect ear for music; this faculty and an inborn facility to play an instrument resulted in his becoming a good musician early in life. He certainly was aware of this talent, but he seemed not to put much value on its further development. He was much more attracted by the adventures of the highway with its changing picture of sunshine and rain, and the lure of the unknown, common to all bohemians. What then, could music hold for him? It only served as a means to earn a livelihood along the road; it prevented him from coming into too close contact with the police; it provided him with an opportunity for adventure. And his instrument was the means of expressing grief and joy which otherwise would have remained mute. The American army recruiting office in New York either did not need musicians, or Krieghoff himself thought that he would find better possibilities in painting than in music. If this had not been so, one would have been inclined to forecast—notwithstanding the danger inherent in all such prophecies—that Krieghoff, instead of becoming a painter, would have made a famous military orchestra leader. His marches and soldiers' songs might well have been the pride of the army even today. The recruiting officer, however, decided to enrol Cornelius as a military draftsman, and in so doing determined his future career.

Hundreds of sketches and pictures, faithfully produced as commanded, contributed to shape Cornelius's style and routine. Above all, they made the young man conscious of the fact that this kind of activity was eminently suited to answer to all his economic needs. This problem never left him during his period of wanderings; it had accompanied him on landing in New York; it became a dire necessity when he married. How can I look after my family? The answer must be provided by brush and pen, both of which had already proved their mettle.

Notwithstanding the spontaneous and sincere hospitality that Krieghoff enjoyed in the home of his in-laws, he soon realised that the broad St. Lawrence River which separates Longueuil from Montreal was also a barrier to the possibilities offered by this rapidly growing commercial city. That is why he decided to take up residence in Montreal, where he rented a very modest home of only two rooms for himself, his wife and child, and started painting in all earnest. It has to be said that Cornelius was not a lazy man. Probably already in Toronto, but certainly in Longueuil, he had industriously used his palette.

Louise Gauthier, the lovely country girl, had a true French-Canadian nature and was therefore entirely different from Cornelius; she felt strong ties with the soil of her own country and had all the qualities of the real settler. It is not surprising, then, that although they met and fell in love in New York, they decided both to live on Canadian soil. In the home of the Gauthier family there was little money but life was pleasant and food was always abundant. Without a doubt, these Gauthiers must have been models of kindness and willingness to help. Father Gauthier was well-beloved in the neighbourhood and known by the pet Indian name of 'Vieux Lapokane' (Old Smoke). So far Cornelius, who until the present had been obliged to play his fiddle for the benefit of others, had not been accustomed to this type of mellow and kind humanity. His contact with the older man must have evoked memories of his own childhood, and it was doubtless a revelation to him to find a type of man so different from those he had met on the road of his wanderings. It cannot be said that Cornelius possessed an excessive portion of German sentimentality—so particularly evident in the Southern part of that country. Nevertheless, this first opportunity to truly relax must have impressed him very deeply; otherwise we find it impossible to explain how it is that from this period onwards he developed a real and deep love for the country of his choice. His brother Ernst, in Toronto, remained a German, but Cornelius, as far as possible, assimilated the character of the French-Canadian.

Paradoxically, one might say that this assimilation took place in real 'German fashion', since it was so thorough that Krieghoff himself felt it to be real.

The difference between Cornelius and many other painters now shows up; he paints without the intention of achieving artistic fame. Like many others, he paints in order to provide the wherewithal for his family, but from the very beginning he does not depict fantasies. First, Longueuil provides him with sufficient subjects in his immediate neighbourhod. The peasant-folk and other simple people, the so-called 'habitant' with his cart, horses, and homeliness, and his everyday activities, are portrayed on the canvas. Apart from this, at a distance of a few miles, there is the Indian settlement of Caughnawaga with its population of Iroquois, still preserving their old customs although gradually their mode of life has become almost 'white'.

One is tempted to say that Krieghoff photographs his models and landscapes, but one feels that with each stroke of his brush he has added something very personal: he had captured the most expressive gestures of men and beasts, and their harmonious relation with the homes, woods, mountains and the sum total of the landscape. This technique is possibly produced by an unreasoning intuitional approach and might be the secret of his compellingly dramatic art. If we contemplate his pictures purely from the aspect of painting technique, we do not find much beyond the retarded romanticism he brought with him from Düsseldorf and Schwienfurt, and the schooling obtained in Rotterdam under the influence of Pieter Breughel's canvases. He was not the kind of painter who allows himself to wrestle with new forms of expression and with modern discoveries in colour technique. After settling on his style, he maintained it with remarkable consistency throughout the course of his life, even when in later years he practised his art in France under entirely different conditions. True, his art developed, his untiring activity led to development of technique and style. But his was not the kind of expression which develops in the painter's soul; the changes were due to the larger experience of life through the years.

Thus is becomes clear that his heart did not harbour titanic plans and projects as happens with many artists of greater and less importance. The range of his subjects does not alter. The centre of expression remained, as always, the scenes of everyday life of the French-Canadians with their colourful dresses and costumes of the time, projected into their warm, limpid landscapes. The only difference was that the outer edge of his circle of vision was somewhat enlarged, in order to capture a new version and a new experience. Whatever he has painted, apart from the style which was so much his own, produces a foreign impression—as in his portraits. Notwithstanding his able performance, one often looks for his signature on these works in order to be sure that he actually produced them.

With all this we have rushed somewhat ahead, but it will help to give us a better understanding of the young painter and recently married man; the nomad who suddenly settled down into routine French-Canadian conditions. At the same time we will better understand the revolution which these tremendous changes must have produced in his mind.

At his poor home on Belmont Street near famous Beaverhall in Montreal, the walls were covered with his pictures of the lives of Longueuil settlers, and of landscape lines with the elm trees which bordered on the mighty St. Lawrence. If you had lived at that time, you would often have come across the artist in the old commercial section of the city, carrying a number of his paintings and hunting for customers. He had no other choice, as poverty was a well-known guest in his home. Certainly there was enough ready money in the prosperous city of Montreal to buy all his pictures; but the newly-rich had not assimilated sufficient culture to appreciate an art such as Krieghoff produced. For this, good taste and tradition are essential, and the majority of ostentatious fur traders and lumber merchants held the opinion that paintings were useless nonsense; only a minority showed interest for imported art products representing resounding names, and they lacked the ability to distinguish the real product from the fake. Such people had only recently emerged from the condition of settlers, and it seemed quite repellent to them to cover their modern walls with pictures, thereby reminding them of their former condition of life! Nevertheless, let us give due credit to this society; for however mesmerised by profitable business deals they were, yet our artist made a few sales and obtained some orders. These orders, however, were by no means the kind that he would have liked to obtain. He had to portray teams of horses imported from England; he was asked to sketch pieces of furniture; and sometimes (as in the Place d'Armes) he had to produce signs for new business and bank buildings.

Such slender sources of income could not cover his needs and those of his family, even when they had the opportunity to cross the river every now and then, to appease an excessive hunger at the table of their in-laws. It might have ended very badly for the young family if fate had not kindly taken a hand. It so happened that Cornelius met an Anglo-Canadian who will forever have the distinction of 'discovering' Krieghoff's art and of promoting his work amongst French-Canadians. John Budden met Krieghoff for the first time in Montreal in the year 1851. It seems to happen to most people —and Krieghoff was no exception—that when fortune is kind to them for the first time, they try to thwart it. Apparently Krieghoff was in a queer mood that day, and during his meeting with Budden he showed a retiring and even dismissing attitude. It is hard to explain why the unknown, hungry painter was so blunt when meeting a young but wealthy and very distinguished descendant from an old aristocratic British family. There seems to have been no motive for such an attitude, as John Budden had learned about Krieghoff and approached him in a friendly manner with the purpose of getting to know him and his art. Budden did not live in Montreal; he was a resident of Quebec, the city with the ancient citadel and historical homes, actually the real cradle of the settlement and development of the whole colony. This city, which honoured many old French traditions, did not always look with too much favour on the mushroom growth of Montreal, well on the way to become a metropolis. Krieghoff apparently did not know that the traditional climate of Quebec was more favourable towards his portrayal of Canadian home life than the commercial centre of Montreal, deeply engrossed as it was with profits.

John Budden, with his qualifications of British aristocrat and citizen of Quebec, was part and parcel of this atmosphere. The right kind of contact between both men was not made during the first meeting, but nevertheless Budden bought a few of Krieghoff's smaller pictures and took them with him to Quebec. The prices Krieghoff asked for these pictures varied from five to ten dollars apiece—stark irony when one knows that today a good picture by Krieghoff, if obtainable at all, fetches anything between four and five thousand dollars. John Budden was particularly impressed by Krieghoff's landscapes of Canadian winters, even though these pictures had not attained at that time the high level of accomplishment they were to reach about six years later. This later perfection is due not only to the improved technique of the artist. Winter in the wide, damp plains of Montreal—located on an unmistakable climatic frontier—often shows mist and does not produce the crystal brilliancy and the superb splendour of winter near Quebec. Also, Montreal does not have a wide background of mountains, nor the impressive, deeply-carved riverbeds of the tributaries of the St. Lawrence, so striking a feature of the Quebec area. All this must have contributed to the fact that the accent in his pictures produced during the Montreal period is rather on the foreground, on the people that are portrayed and their accessories. The landscape as such does not mean much more than a necessary background, like the wings of a theatre within which the action takes place. It was only after the artist settled himself in Quebec that the more penetrating values of the landscape became of equal importance in the scenes he painted.

It was not until two years later, in 1853, that Krieghoff met Budden again. In the meantime things had gone from bad to worse for the artist. He changed his address often, possibly because he could not meet the rent, and finally, to keep himself and his family afloat, he got himself a job as a housepainter. When matters could not have been worse, he received a visit from John Budden. This time the meeting took place under better conditions, as apparently Krieghoff acted normally and did not hide his situation. According to contemporary witnesses, Budden took a real liking to Cornelius and treated him somewhat as a big child, to be led by the hand. Krieghoff gives the impression of egocentrism, and as entirely wrapped up in his own affairs. He had not relinquished his part of the German romanticism of his younger days, and this type of man lives inwardly; he tries to avoid meeting beyond the necessities of daily existence; he wanders along the highways of life without understanding hard facts. Budden was exactly the opposite type; he was a society man through and through, an extrovert for whom human relations were the salt of the life. It was not only a matter of two extremes being attracted; there must have been a bridge of understanding between both men apart from painting, of which admittedly Budden did not understand very much. It was likely a trait both men had in common; both were loyal and above-board, the type of man a Britisher would call a good fellow, if not a gentleman.

Budden noticed Krieghoff's plight from the start, and he keenly perceived that much could be made out of Cornelius in Quebec; therefore he suggested to him on the spot that he take up residence there, and come to live in his own home. There was room to spare; Budden was a bachelor and the small Krieghoff family would find plenty of accommodation. Krieghoff immediately accepted the offer; he saw a new hope and felt a revival of his longing in response to the call of the road. For Louise, things were much more difficult. Despite all the misery, she felt herself at home within the well-known boundaries. She had her kind parents and many good friends in or near Montreal, whereas Quebec was foreign territory, of which she had more than her share during their sojourn in

New York. Moreover, Krieghoff's brother Ernst had left Toronto and taken up residence in Montreal. It took many hours of council with relatives and friends before the couple actually made the decision to leave their present surroundings and to embark upon an unknown future in Quebec. They tried, however, to persuade Ernst to join them in the adventure, together with his wife Susanna and their three children. But Ernst did not, apparently, possess the same bohemian inclinations as his brother. He was a good draftsman himself, but did not practise an art unable to provide him with a living; he worked instead as a cabinet-maker in Montreal, and earned a decent living at this conservative trade. He had also become a member of the German clubs already in existence at that time, and did not feel inclined to separate himself from friends made there.

Upon arrival in Quebec Krieghoff, his wife Louise and their daughter Emilie, were very kindly received in the relatively small but comfortable cottage on Mount Pleasant owned by Budden. Who can say what thoughts crossed Cornelius's mind as he stepped over the threshold of his new home for the first time? He certainly could not foresee that he would spend nearly the rest of his life here, and that the feverish activity previously necessitated by poverty would find its reward from now on. Neither would he know that the shadow of death was travelling with them and that within a few years the quiet, courageous partner of his long period of anxiety would be taken away. Unconsciously he had already dedicated to his wife the fairest monument that a painter can create. As early as in the paintings of his Montreal period, in the 1843 'Canadian Settlers Playing Cards' you will notice a beautiful young woman in the background, carrying a baby girl of about two years of age. It is his wife and little daughter. Over and over again until her early death she was his model, and in almost all his pictures portraying the life of French-Canadian settlers we shall find her lovely figure and long, pale face with the big, almond-shaped eyes, which remind us of famous Italian pictures. The fact is extraordinary in view of the eagerness of most painters to find new models.

From the first day onwards Budden took his self-created task as mentor and protector very seriously. Apparently he had more confidence in the value of Cornelius's art than the painter himself. To start with, he took Krieghoff on tours around Quebec—to the Montmorency Falls, the Indian settlements of Loretto, and many other unusual sights, in order to show the artist that subjects were much more numerous and impressive than around Montreal. The contrast between the flat expanses of the river area at Montreal and the hinterland of Quebec with its deep woods and the Laurentian mountains with their wild rivers cutting deep furrows in the slopes, soon became evident. Apart from all this, Krieghoff felt the strong appeal of the gay and carefree existence of Quebec society, not dominated by fur traders and other merchants but by officers and officials of the city. There were already literary and dramatic circles, and painting was held in certain esteem. Looking backwards from our own perspective, at that time Quebec was the only city on the North American continent, inclusive the United States, which provided an atmosphere permitting artists like Krieghoff to breathe and relax. This does not at all mean that Quebec was waiting for Krieghoff with open arms. Here too, there was only a thin layer of society interested in the arts. As far as painting was concerned, those professing any interest were still very far from the sentiment of 'Art for Art's sake'. Photography was still in its infancy and painting was looked upon as a trade, useful for portraying a person in a Victorian pose well 'decorated' with rich materials, and with a background of vines. There was, however, an undercurrent quite favourable for Krieghoff's art. History had chosen Quebec as the stronghold of French-Canadian nationalism. It was therefore evident that Quebec would favour pictorial expression of the life of its own people, and would cherish such pictures against imported products of art. True, the barriers of class distinction have often retarded the development of this tendency, but here another and somewhat more banal motive favoured Krieghoff. The British officers stationed in Quebec bought his pictures to send home as souvenirs for the benefit of their relatives and friends.

Budden, moreover, was a keen businessman, and one must judge his interest in Krieghoff—as it was only normal—partly from this angle. Budden was a partner of the firm of Maxham and Co. in Quebec, and he induced them to advertise Krieghoff's art and to arrange auctions of his pictures. He also introduced Krieghoff to his numerous friends and invited them to come and visit the studio of the artist. The most important explanation of Krieghoff's quick popularity, however, was his ability to adapt himself rapidly to the customs of the city; which were at that time fairly rough but full of life and colour. He had a large variety of anecdotes and jokes to tell; he danced beautifully; he was a valuable partner on hunting expeditions since his excellent eyesight gave him perfect aim. He could hold his own in any company, even at drinking parties, many of which specialised in serving strong gin in tall wine glasses. If during a festival the musicians grew tired, Krieghoff would immediately take up an instrument and delight the party with his musical ability. The strongest incentive to his extraordinary zeal must have been seeing all those wealthy, satisfied people, without having a nickel himself. He must have felt like a Bajazzo, an outsider, and he made no secret of it; he would confess to his new friends: 'I have to work to earn money'. Budden succeeded in making Krieghoff what might be called the 'fashion of the day' by a clever bit of adroitness. The Governor-General, Lord Elgin, had arrived in Quebec for an official visit. Krieghoff had already met his lordship two years before on the latter's passing through Longueuil. Budden arranged that Krieghoff, armed with a portfolio, was located at a spot where Elgin could not avoid seeing him. His lordship passed, recognised him and spoke to him, mentioning that he would like to see his pictures. Budden then cleverly contrived that Lord Elgin should make an appointment with Krieghoff to visit his studio. The bystanders naturally had listened to the conversation, and the news that the Governor-General had promised to visit the painter went through the city like wildfire. All of a sudden impulse, every-body in Quebec who had a distinguished name and money discovered that it was fashionable to visit Krieghoff's studio.

These indeed were great days in the life of the painter, and they meant a great deal to Budden too. From now on they could feel certain that they had vanquished the social strong-hold of Quebec. Krieghoff was not slow in appreciating the change and painted like one possessed. Probably he took not more than a single day over his smaller pictures and sold them with the paint still wet. Nevertheless, the prices he obtained improved only very slowly. His success came only by dint of hard work. According to conservative estimates Krieghoff must have painted about seven hundred pictures in Canada, amongst which were many duplicates. Many of these must have been destroyed by fire, particularly the one which ravaged Quebec in the year 1881; nevertheless, it has been possible to date to find nearly five hundred pictures, both originals and duplicates, painted by Krieghoff, and these have been carefully listed.

In order to improve his earnings, Krieghoff also taught painting. Furthermore, art dealers in the United States started to take an interest in his typical Canadian art. He received orders from New York firms for pictures, which were subse-quently reproduced in the States as cheaply-coloured litho-graphs. The best known prints still adorn the walls of many American homes; they bear the titles 'For the Sake of God's Mercy', and 'To Hell with You'. Both pictures represent an old Canadian beggar; one portrays him receiving an abundant gift, the other as chasing a miser who had refused to give him anything at all. His skill and the encouragement of popular success quickly brought Krieghoff to the heights of his artistic ability. Along with a large number of pictures produced with feverish haste for the marked or private orders, he now also created genuine works of art which represent his appreciation for the manner in which Quebec took to him, and which will remain the perpetual pride of that city. This applies to the whole of French Canada, of which he has pictured landscape, people, and customs during an important period of its historical development. It would be wrong to assume that Krieghoff developed his qualities as a painter only in Quebec. His individual way of observing, conceiving, and finally reproducing the result with his brush was determined by his own nature and developed by his contact with the Gauthier family. His poverty before the Quebec period may have retarded his development, but even then some of his pictures seem to tear aside the dark curtains of his grief and show the high degree of talent he possessed. In 1851 he painted chiefly business signs for banks and taverns, but in between such commissions he also managed to produce 'The Hostelry of the White Horse in Moonlight'. The brown, wooden construction of the hostelry stands at the edge of a deep wood, of which the endless rows of firs disappear in the distance into the faint mist of a winter evening. There has been a light fall of snow on the roads; a warm light flows from the windows of the house. A sleigh waits at the door of the inn; in the background a nearly full moon shines through the clouds; the pale moonlight blends with the red and orange colours produced by light from the hostelry and shows up the tracks of the sleigh, which disappear into the woods. The mastery of the effect of light, learned in Holland and clearly shown in this picture, is typical of the future master of the Canadian landscape. His 'Winter Landscape', produced in 1849, may be admired in the National Gallery at Ottawa. It takes us to the shores of the St. Lawrence and impresses by the wide horizon of the river expanse. A sparse, thin, wintry wood and a distant chain of hills provide the boundaries of the picture. On the left side, where the forest begins, you see the home of a settler which the painter has adorned with a walled fireplace, probably a result of his own partiality for this detail. A red, peasant sleigh with a white horse impatiently looking down upon a small barking dog, shows up very clearly against the background of the picture. The two small figures in the sleigh, well wrapped up against the cold, are a young woman and a small girl: Krieghoff's wife and daughter. His wife is apparently using an imported Scottish rug for the covering. Two men, also wearing regional costumes, and the children standing behind the sleigh, seem to form part of the Gauthier family. The picture is of great interest in that it shows the talent of the painter along with certain defects, which seem to have been vanquished two years later when he produced his 'Hostelry of the White Horse in Moonlight'. It reveals that the improvement of his talent had already begun in his Montreal period.

Krieghoff reached the height of his career in 1856 with the picture 'Playing Time in the Village School'. We are once more given a wintry landscape. The red sleigh of a settler, drawn by a brown horse, has apparently advanced from the village in the left background, and crosses a frozen brook towards the highway. This seems to lead us to two tall picturesque firs towards the school, located on a small elevation in the foreground. Immediately above, the sky has the typical clearness of winter, but in the distance white masses of clouds traverse the scene. Near the school we find a number of frolicking, gambolling children throwing snowballs; the scene is full of movement and entirely natural; it reminds us of Pieter Breughel. The picture contains nothing which could be attributed to the painter's fancy, and the homes and human figures show no imported accessories. What we actually see are the typical Canadian settlers' homes of the period, the sleighs used in the country, and the people dressed in their authentic costumes. This picture, which is private property, but which we should like to see in the National Gallery, is a sincere document of settler life in Canada, and it tells us more about this life than we can learn from thick history books. In 1856 Krieghoff painted 'After the Ball', which provides an amusing and faithful portrayal of social life during the winter season in Quebec. Anybody interested in studying the life and customs of Quebec people during the Victorian period, will do well to study this picture with full attention.

In 1854 Krieghoff and his small family started on a voyage which took them by way of England and Paris to his native country. What could have been his reason for the trip? Quebec fully appreciated his talent, but obviously European art and the talents of European artists, and French art in particular, were often topics of discussion. It seems that Budden was the first to suggest the voyage, since from a commercial viewpoint he saw certain advantages in Krieghoff's prolonged absence, and probably expected a favourable advance in his talent through the influence of foreign study. It is unknown whether the painter had the same expectations as Budden, but it is likely that he appreciated the value of Budden's arguments, and assumed that his voyage might increase his standing as an artist and increase the volume of his sales. Apart from all this, he felt that it would be well to have a personal contact with art dealers in London, with whom he had been in contact for some time in connection with the sale of his paintings. And finally, one can easily understand that he desired to visit the places of his uncertain early years. The Krieghoff family remained in Paris about two months, and here Krieghoff sold his herbarium of Canadian plants, carefully collected over the course of the years. Apparently he was a very capable botanist. After arranging this sale, he immediately began to paint in the Louvre. He made copies of many masterpieces, but also produced several originals. The most impressive of his own works at that time is a picture of his wife dressed in Italian style, and presented as a peasant woman harvesting grapes.

There is not much information obtainable on their later visit to Germany. It seems that they visited Düsseldorf and other places further south. Krieghoff was not so fascinated by Europe that he contemplated settling there, as was feared by some of his friends, and after an absence of seven or eight months we find him back at his easel in Budden's home in Quebec. It is impossible to say whether or not the trip had matured Krieghoff's art and whether it was a deception or a gain. One thing, however, is certain: the voyage had produced no change in direction from the road on which he had started in Longueuil. Schiller had one time written: 'When the road is taken, the goal is reached'; it was very true for Krieghoff.

The portrayal of regional Canadian scenes, mostly in a wintry landscape, remained his aim to the end of his life.

In his younger years Krieghoff had excellent teachers and a great eagerness to learn. We have already mentioned that he was a capable botanist and had succeeded in making a systematic collection of plants in accordance with scientific requirements. Furthermore, he was no stranger to the chemistry of colour, and although he used prepared paints he himself often prepared what he needed. The procedure he used remained his own professional secret. Many of his pictures, which have only recently been cleaned by taking off the layers of dust and soot, look as if they had been produced last week, so fresh are the colours. In isolated cases he made mistakes in his mixtures, and sometimes, over the course of the years, a clear red colour had darkened to a dull ochre, to the disadvantage of the picture's character. This, however, does provide proof that he experimented with his own colours.

Of the series of beautiful and impressive works produced after the return from Europe, the 'Log Cabin of a Settler', painted in 1856, and 'Winter in Quebec' (1860) deserve special attention. The log cabin in the wintry landscape of the Laurentian Mountains is a real monument to the pioneering settler, who pitched his strength against the wilderness of the northern woods. From a valley on a higher level we look down on a vast perspective of woods covering the slopes of endless hills. Above, the sky is high, stormy and cloudy, and foreshadows the coming of spring. At the outer edge of the brown and green woods, in the foreground and to the left of the observer, the cabin made of roughly hewn logs stands in the snow in the yellow daylight. The brook on the right is still frozen. The settler's wife, a small child in her arms, stands at the door, whilst her husband unloads wood from the ox-drawn sleigh. In the snow in front of the house are a number of scattered tools, and the other children play nearby. The picture is a reproduction of the conditions of existence of the settlers which obtained in the Canadian woods around the year 1850.

'Winter in Quebec' gives us a picture of a Canadian village in the same period, and in the same landscape. In the centre of the canvas you find the home-made, horse-drawn sleigh of the settler riding fast; three men are in it, wearing the colourful costumes of that time.

Krieghoff was not only active as a painter in Quebec, as has been already intimated. He was a member of a dramatic circle and of several other associations partly aesthetic and partly social. The tall, slender man, slightly grey already, was well liked; he was an accomplished dancer, a good talker, a capable hunter and a sportsman, and probably a congenial drinker as well. There were only very few old-fashioned and puritan families that failed to find the artist fully 'acceptable' after having observed him in the Quebec streets with his never-changing velvet clothes and round beaver cap. Possibly these over-sensitive ears had also heard that although the artist was well aware of the value of money, and was continually trying to make it, yet he was quite capable of spending the income of many weeks of hard work at his easel, in a single night.

In 1858 his beloved wife passed away after a short illness during a visit to relatives in Longueuil. She died as quietly as she had lived with him during many years. The misfortune seems to have hit the artist much deeper than could be noticed by his friends. He was perhaps too sensitive to show his feelings, knowing that man is often too callous and egoistical to understand his fellow—of whose qualities Krieghoff himself had learned much during his lifetime. He bore his grief silently and outwardly appeared undisturbed. Even the most polished sophisticate, however, would not have been able to hide such a serious misfortune entirely. Krieghoff reacted by dedicating himself to his work as he had never done before. But memories of the kind helpmate during so many years of hardship up to the Quebec period of success, haunted him and finally came to dominate his thoughts. His creative power and artistic intuition rapidly diminished. His loneliness increased when his daughter, for her second marriage, left him to take up residence in Chicago with her husband, a Russian count. Later, in 1867, he accepted her invitation and went to Chicago himself. Once more, in 1871, he paid a short visit to Quebec. The following year, back in Chicago, he passed away suddenly.

EPILOGUE

In accordance with the aim of the author, the little book you have been reading was written particularly for those who have had no previous experience of Canadian art and literature. It had to be composed, therefore, without any particular premise. It appeared to the author that a good introduction would comprise a mosaic of short biographies explaining the artistic product through the portrait of their creator and in addition, within wide boundaries, by describing the centre and the country to which they belong. The danger of this procedure was that the usual cliché of the condensed history of art and literature seemed unavoidable. If that system had been adopted, the author would have had no freedom to choose those amongst Canadian artists who represent interesting facts of this extraordinary country through their personality or their fate.

In discarding the scientific thoroughness of the complete history book, the necessity to juggle dates, years and quotations disappeared, and both author and readers are left equally free from that ballast. The reader who needs such details for specific study will find them in the professional literature on the subject, of which a condensed list is annexed. As a result, it has been possible to shape our facts more compactly in this little book, and to show the ties of art and literature with everyday life. Obviously, a first introduction can only contain the historical background and the fundamentals of the subject; for this reason only artists and poets of obvious historical significance have been mentioned. The portrayal of modern Canadian art and literature has been reserved for a later volume.

The author has not hesitated to express his own opinions in the present work. A honest confession on this point seemed to be more useful to the reader than a vague neutrality. Another motive for this attitude was that in the early period of Canadian art and literature, the country itself, its people and its history, represented the real focus of all artistic creation. Modern art, and that which is called modern literature—both with their clear tendencies towards 'l'art pour l'art', are cosmopolitan, and as such, separated from the soil of their creation. They can tell us only very little about the country of their origin, which again would not have served the purpose of this book.

It should not be thought that the older form of the arts in Canada is dead. A large number of contemporary and active poets and authors, painters and sculptors, remained faithful to what might be called the humanistic trend. The battle that is continuing in order to discover the future trend of Canadian letters, has in no way been decided. The impressive and heroic nature of this country has not been tamed by mankind to the extent of ceasing to exercise a strong influence on the future development of sensibility. The noise of machinery gone mad, created by Man himself, cannot permanently succeed in drowning the solemn, grandiose symphony of Nature. This is evident enough when it is realised that Man likes to keep this machinery clamouring near him. This does not mean in any way, however, that the voice of Nature and the voice of God in Nature, have ceased to exist. In this sense, there will be full understanding for a recommendation given by the Canadian poet and Minister P. J. O. Chauveau to Canadian authors and artists during the ceremony of foundation of the 'French Canadian Institute', contained in the following words: 'You experience in a way more vivid than I could express, the full magic of the birth of literature in a new country. If, so far, you have not done so, then it will be sufficient to glance at the exertions of older and duller nations, to find undiscovered roads and new horizons. You have so many powerful elements of success in your hands: scenes of a wild life which gradually disappears; a civilisation which is being born; a majestic and fairly unknown Nature; the heroic battles of our ancestors; and captivating and admirable characters and customs, of which still so little has been used in the sketches of your predecessors. All these things represent an untouched heritage to you, and you should hasten to use them profitably and to their full extent.'

Chauveau is a French-Canadian and of course he addresses his French-Canadian compatriots and—no doubt—in the same sense also the English-Canadian compatriots, because 'the past glories of this country are in a very particular way his glories, the glories of his own people, the pioneers, religious and laiety, who came to this country when it was wilderness. But cannot the English-Canadian, without being able to delve so deeply into the past, derive some inspiration from the past of this country? Should they not take equal pride with their French-Canadian compatriots in the heroism and devotion of the Jesuit Fathers—in Dollard, in Champlain and Jacques Cartier? Why should Canadian history start for them with the Battle of the Plains of Abraham and not with Jacques Cartier's first voyage up the St. Lawrence?'[1]

[1] *The Montreal Star*, September 22nd, 1951, p. 8.

HISTORICAL TABLE

1534 Cartier arrives at the St. Lawrence River
1603 First French settlement in Nova Scotia
1608 Foundation of Quebec by Champlain
1668 Mgr. Laval founds the School of Arts and Handicrafts
in Quebec
1678 Father Hennepin at Niagara Falls
1742–1749 Construction of the Church of the Holy Family on
Orleans Island near Quebec
1759 Conquest by the British
1776 American Revolution
1780 Death of the first painter born in Canada, Abbot
J. A. Aide-Crequy
1780–1812 Immigration of English Loyalists
1802–1823 Louise Quevillon and his School of Art in Montreal
1812–1814 War with the United States
1837 The Papineau Revolt
1860 Foundation of the Society of Arts in Montreal
1871 Death of the painter Paul Kane
1872 Death of the painter Cornelius Krieghoff
1880 Foundation of the Canadian National Gallery
1885 First railway communication between the Atlantic and
Pacific
1913 Edition of the first Yearbook of Art in Canada
1927 Exhibition of Canadian Art in Paris
1937 The Coronation Exhibition in London
1938 'A Century of Canadian Art', Tate Gallery, London

BIBLIOGRAPHY

Jean Bruchesi, *Histoire du Canada pour tous*

W. D. Buchanan, *James Wilson Morrice*

W. W. Campbell, *Oxford Book of Canadian Verse*, Oxford–Toronto, 1913

Canadian Poets, *Anthology*, Garvin, Toronto, 1926

Marcel Dugas, *Littérature canadienne*

J. Fournier et O. Asselin, *Anthologie des poètes canadiens*, Montreal, 1920

C. ab der Halden, *Études de littérature canadienne-française*, Quebec, 1904
Nouvelles études de littérature canadienne-française, Montreal, 1907

M. O. Hammond, *Painting and Sculpture in Canada*

J. Huston, *Répertoire national ou recueil de littérature canadienne*, 4 vols., Montreal, 1848–50

H. James, *Bibliography of Canadian Literature*, Toronto, 1899

Edmond Lareau, *Histoire de la littérature canadienne*

MacMechan, *Headwaters of Canadian Literature*, Toronto, 1925

MacMurchy, *Canadian Literature*, Toronto, 1906

Newton McTavish, *The Fine Arts in Canada*

Olivier Maurault, *L'art au Canada*

Albert H. Robson, *Canadian Landscape Painters*

William Smith, *History of Canada from its first discovery to the Peace of 1763*

E. C. Woodley, *The Province of Quebec through Four Centuries*

INDEX OF NAMES

Aide-Crequy, J. A., 171

Balzac, Honoré, 22
Bibaud, Michel, 15
Bienville, François, 25, 30
Bigot, François, 27, 36
Bougainville, 14
Bourinot, John, 114
Budden, John, 155

Cabot, 36
Carman, 64
Cartier, Jacques, 36, 170, 171
Casgrain, Abbé, 52
Champlain, Samuel, 9, 36, 170, 171
Charles the Great, 12
Châteaubriand, 65
Chauveau, Joseph, 22, 169
Cooper, Fenimore, 41
Coté, Jean-Baptiste, 17
Crane, Stephen, 65
Crawford, Isabella, 64
Crémazie, Octave, 15, 45
Cullen, Maurice, 140

Dante, Alighieri, 134
Dow-Lighthall, William, 15
Dumas, Alexandre, 27, 31

Ferland, Abbé, 49
Flaubert, G., 65
France, Anatole, 85
Frazer, Forbes, 64
Fréchette, Louis, 16, 31, 33

Galt, John, 41, 101
Garland, Hamlin, 65
Garneau, Alfred, 49
Gauldrée-Boileau, 49
Gauthier, Louise, 149, 152
Garneau, François Xavier, 22
Gill, Charles, 120
Gobineau, Count, 12
Goethe, J. W., 24, 32
Goldsmith, Oliver, 43
Guizot, François, 22

Haliburton, 110
Harrison, John L., 18
Heavysege, Charles, 64
Hebert, Philippe, 17
Hemon, Louis, 85
Howe, Joseph, 118

Ingres, Jean-Dominique, 143

Jacobi, O. R., 17
Jolliet, 35

Kalm, Baron, 14, 40
Kane, Paul, 16, 137, 171
Keats, 69, 71
Kirby, William, 15, 34
Krieghoff, Cornelius, 16, 17, 137, 148, 171

Lampman, 64, 81
La Salle, 35
Laval, Mgr., 171
La Verendrye, 35
Locke, 102
London, Jack, 65
Louis XIV, 35, 88
Louis XV, 35

MacDougall, 73
Macculoe, 18
Mair, Charles, 63
Marmette, Joseph, 20, 22, 23
Marx, Karl, 85
Matisse, 146
Michelet, Jules, 22
Milton, 43
Moodie, Susanna, 99
Morrice, James W., 17, 137

Parr, Catherine, 101
Peel, Paul, 17

Pelham, Edgar, 100
Phipps, 23
Plamondon, Antoine, 17
Poe, Edgar Allan, 41
Pope, Alexander, 43, 70

Quésnel, Joseph, 14
Quévillon, Louise, 171

Repentigny, 40
Richardson, John, 15
Riel, 65
Roberts, Charles, 64, 79, 81
Rousseau, J.-J., 65

Sangster, Charles, 15, 64, 66, 113, 140
Scott, Walter, 41
Socrates, 46
Steffens, Lincoln, 65
Strickland, Thomas, 101, 113
Suzor-Coté, Aurel, 17, 140

Taché, Etienne Pascal, 21
Turner, William, 143

Voltaire, 22

Zola, Emile, 85